Adirondack Furniture and the Rustic Tradition

Adirondack Furniture

and the Rustic Tradition ≫ Craig Gilborn

Harry N. Abrams, Inc., Publishers ≫ New York

PROJECT DIRECTOR: MARGARET L. KAPLAN

EDITOR: ERIC HIMMEL

DESIGNER: ELISSA ICHIYASU

AN EARLIER VERSION OF THE SECTION ON INDIANA HICKORY (PP. 240–251)

ORIGINALLY APPEARED IN *ARTS & ANTIQUES* (JANUARY–FEBRUARY 1981).

LIBRARY OF CONGRESS CATALOGING-IN-PUBLICATION DATA

GILBORN, CRAIG A.

ADIRONDACK FURNITURE AND THE RUSTIC TRADITION.

BIBLIOGRAPHY: P. 335

INCLUDES INDEX.

1. COUNTRY FURNITURE—NEW YORK (STATE)

—ADIRONDACK MOUNTAINS—HISTORY—19TH CENTURY.

2. COUNTRY FURNITURE—NEW YORK (STATE)

—ADIRONDACK MOUNTAINS—HISTORY—20TH CENTURY.

3. FOLK ART—NEW YORK (STATE)—ADIRONDACK MOUNTAINS.

I. TITLE.

NK2435.N7G55   1987   749.2147′53   87-1381

ISBN 0-8109-1844-7

1 (frontispiece)

The porch at Trophy Lodge, Brandreth Park, c. 1890.

The table in the photograph (figure 107) was found by the author

in 1974 less than fifteen feet from this location

To Alice

Contents

Cottage and Bungalow Furniture

From Old-Time Rustic Workers to Contemporary Craftsmen

2

Rustic shelters on Mohonk
Lake, Mohonk Mountain
House, Ulster County,
New York, 1879 and later

T he preparation of this book has taken me thirteen years. To the many who helped, I here acknowledge my debt, with thanks.

The following individuals: Ted Aber, Mrs. Morison Garrett Brigham, Knox Burger, Mr. and Mrs. Allen Dines, Robert Doyle, Mr. and Mrs. E. I. du Pont, Mrs. Kenneth Durant, Mr. and Mrs. Richard Fay, Wen Fong, Mr. and Mrs. George Fuge, Heidi Fuge, Mr. and Mrs. Anthony N. B. Garvan, Marge Lamy, Richard Lawrence, Peter and Rosine Lemon, Suellen Linn, Coy Ludwig, David Luthy, Mary Jean Madigan, Michael Palmer, Clarence and William Petty, Mr. and Mrs. Whitelaw Reid, Nancy E. Richards, Gordon Saltar, Marcia Smith, Frank H. Sommers, Mr. and Mrs. Roland Stearns, Mr. and Mrs. Howard Stewart, Holman J. Swinney, Neville Thompson, Mr. and Mrs. Carter Walker, Sidney Whelan, Jr., Richard Wright, and Carl deZeeuw.

Museums whose furniture is illustrated in this book are credited in the captions. Individuals and other institutions are credited at the end. They all contributed to the final appearance of this book, and I wish to thank them collectively here.

Acknowledgments

People at the following museums, libraries, and other organizations were especially helpful: the Adirondack League Club; Central Park Conservancy, New York City; Essex County Historical Society, Elizabethtown, New York; Netti Marie Jones Fine Arts Library, Lake Placid, New York; Lake Placid–North Elba Historical Society, Lake Placid, New York; North Woods Club, Minerva, New York; Margaret Woodbury Strong Museum, Rochester; SUNY Cortland Outdoor Education Center (Camp Pine Knot), and the College of Environmental Science and Forestry, Syracuse; also the libraries at the Cooper-Hewitt Museum in New York City and the Onondaga Historical Association, Syracuse.

Closer to home are colleagues and friends at the Adirondack Museum who variously gave assistance and encouragement: Karen Lamoree undertook a number of research tasks; Tracy Meehan, the registrar, tolerated the clutter that followed me through the furniture collection, and she was, as always, helpful in obtaining prints from the museum's collection of photographs; Dorothy Swanson, the secretary, patiently typed several versions of the manuscript; Jerold Pepper, the librarian, was always ready to order a needed book from interlibrary loan; and Peter C. Welsh, the curator, demonstrated characteristic understanding and initiative on museum matters that deserved closer attention from me. Others no longer on the staff, but not forgotten, are William Crowley, Sarah Comstock, Janet Youngken McLouth, and especially Ted Comstock, who was chiefly responsible for the design of our 1976 "Adirondack Rustic" exhibition. At Abrams I would like to thank Sam Antupit, Leta Bostelman, Eric Himmel, Elissa Ichiyasu, Margaret Kaplan, and Susan Shapiro.

The founder of the Adirondack Museum, Harold K. Hochschild, and his brother, Walter Hochschild, did not live to see this book published; but Adam Hochschild has been no less supportive than his father and uncle.

The course of this project imposed countless domestic burdens on my wife, Alice Wolf Gilborn. She accepted them with forbearance. It is a measure of her strength of character that during this period she published a book of her own, wrote magazine articles, founded and edited a literary magazine, and conducted several major editorial assignments for the Adirondack Museum, while raising our son, Alexis, and giving birth *(mirabile dictu!)* to our daughter, Amanda.

3

Title page, from
Ideas for Rustic
Furniture
(London, c. 1780)

Trees are as closets from which good woodsmen take whatever they may need.

—Anonymous writer
relating the
Adirondack travels
of two young men
in 1843,
ST. LAWRENCE
PLAINDEALER,
August 24, 1881

4

Young woman seated on a rustic bench, c. 1900. This photograph was found among the effects of C. H. Downs, a taxidermist with business addresses in Blue Mountain Lake, New York, and Lebanon, New Hampshire

T his book had its inception soon after my arrival as director of the Adirondack Museum in 1972 when I first encountered Adirondack furniture. My impression of the furniture's originality was confirmed when Jonathan Fairbanks, a friend and former colleague at the Winterthur Museum, on a social visit, admired a handsome cupboard ornamented with twigs from ten varieties of trees and shrubs, made in the 1880s for Camp Cedars *(figure 205)*. An authority on American furniture, and currently curator at the Museum of Fine Arts in Boston, Fairbanks reinforced my regard for the cupboard and the few other rustic pieces then on display. Thus I began planning "Adirondack Rustic: Camp Furniture, 1876–1926," an exhibition that filled three galleries of the Adirondack Museum in the summer of 1976. That no catalogue accompanied the exhibit, the first of its kind in a museum, was a complaint leveled then and since. But I believed that the subject required further study. Nearly all the furniture and a few of the decorative items in that show have been included in this book, together with many additions, some subsequently donated to the Adirondack Museum.

Introduction

I learned, as does anyone afield in the Adirondacks, that the project demanded time, patience, and a willingness to seize each opportunity. The Adirondack Park is big: it covers a territory about the size of Massachusetts, and those vacation homes in which rustic work was allegedly to be found were upwards of sixty miles from my home and work in Blue Mountain Lake. Some camps were on dirt roads, sometimes far off the highway; others were accessible only by boat; all were occupied only part of the year, which necessitated making appointments for summer while the snow still lay deep on the ground outside my window.

Once admitted, I seldom found one visit satisfactory. Note- and picture-taking were difficult. Having lived in their camps for years, some since childhood, my hosts regarded their summer homes as they might a member of the family, with a complacency that comes from familiarity. We enjoyed one another's sense of discovery—theirs a fresh perspective borrowed from an outsider. Meanwhile, the subjects of my studies were slowly disappearing through neglect or accident. Three of the forty or so camps that I visited in the 1970s have since been de-

stroyed by fire; the photographs in my file, a few of which are reproduced here, may be the only surviving pictorial record of their
furnishings.

This book illustrates as much as half the museum-quality "twiggy"
pieces of Adirondack origin, the majority concentrated at camps within
a ten-mile radius of Raquette Lake, as well as a broad representation
of rustic furniture used in the Adirondack Park. While *Adirondack
Furniture and the Rustic Tradition* is intended to add to the appreciation of a subject about which little has been known, it may also hasten
the dispersal of the very things it praises, making further documenta-
tion in the field that much more difficult. Rustic furniture is now sought
by dealers and collectors who may be disinclined to learn where a piece
was made and used, and under what circumstances. The origin and
history of objects are easily misplaced and, like umbrellas left behind
in restaurants or trains, are seldom reclaimed.

In the absence of published accounts of Adirondack furniture, mis-
conceptions, even among professionals, abound. Dealers and writers
often use the term "Adirondack" in connection with rustic furniture
having nothing to do with the Adirondacks. A bent-willow chair manufactured today in several southern states is called an "Adirondack rustic chair," and a twig basket was said to express "a rustic Adirondack
style." A gateleg table is asserted to have been inspired by "eighteenth-
century Adirondack designs," though the Adirondacks were hardly settled much before 1820. A chair that probably originated in the lower
end of the Hudson River Valley *(figure 82)*, far south of the Adirondacks, is called "American Gothic Adirondack."[1]

Inconsequential in themselves, such references suggest the belief
that rustic work and ideas flowed from the Adirondacks to other parts
of the nation. An example is the statement that the fashion for rustic
furnishings "spread south and west from there [the Adirondacks] to
blanket the whole Appalachian chain, evolving as it went."[2] But there
is no evidence that Adirondack furniture had any measurable influence
on rustic work produced elsewhere; no evidence even that the slatted
chair popularly known as the "Adirondack chair" *(figure 284)* was ever
made in the Adirondacks. Only the Westport chair *(figure 279)* is known
to have originated in the Adirondacks.

An appreciation of Adirondack rustic furniture is possible without
exaggerating the Adirondack contribution. A balanced appraisal awaits
knowledge of rustic work done elsewhere, including the resort areas of
northern New England, the Appalachian states, Michigan, Minnesota,
and Wisconsin, and the Rocky Mountain region and California. If any-

thing comparable is to be found, however, it will likely turn up in Britain and not the United States, for reasons outlined in this book.

Adirondack rustic furniture excels in its variety of forms and techniques. This may be evident to the reader as he looks at the illustrations and the chapter headings in the table of contents. Rustic workers in the region fifty to a hundred years ago used more of the tree more variously than their modern descendants have done to date, and they can be said to have possessed, therefore, a larger rustic vocabulary.

Within that obscure corner of the decorative arts that is set aside for furnishings for the lawn, porch, and camp, a number of Adirondack pieces must be counted among the best. Attention to detail and refinement of expression was not a trait of American rustic work until Adirondack woodsmen started to turn their hands and minds to it in the 1870s. Until then, rustic furniture was generally rough or crude; the Victorians considered it unsuited to use indoors, except perhaps in a dimly lit entrance hall or as a planter in a conservatory or north window. In the Adirondacks, rustic furniture took a giant leap into the house itself. To be sure, this crossing of a barrier took place in a woodland camp and not in a suburban box or country house. But something of importance may be said to have occurred if J. Pierpont Morgan, Collis P. Huntington, and Alfred G. Vanderbilt are among those who used and admired the furniture at their camps. And the charm of the earliest Adirondack camps was favorably noticed a decade before the very rich entered the Adirondack stage.

The novelty and therefore much of the interest for these newcomers was in the rustic furniture and rustic detailing inside the cottages that made up camp enclaves like Camp Pine Knot and Camp Cedars. Rustic furniture did not fill any room, but what was there—a cedar table with mosaic twig top in the center of the room, or a double bed with four bark-covered posts in the corner—heightened the rustic ambience of camp life in a way that excited the sensibilities. That the furniture was appropriate to its setting seems obvious to us, but not to our Victorian predecessors, who were still new to furnishing a home in the woods.

To be acceptable indoors, even in a camp setting, the furniture had to have some degree of comfort and sophistication. This meant avoiding, on the one hand, the crude furniture identified elsewhere on these pages as "ramshackle" (see p. 83), and, on the other, furniture that aspired to a condition above its rustic "station." I can think of no examples of the latter from the Adirondacks, but the furniture of Ernest Stowe marks the limit. A dining table and twelve chairs to match were sold at auction in New York City for $45,000 in December 1986 (figure

5

*Lawn at Windsor
Hotel, Schroon Lake.
Photograph by
Seneca Ray Stoddard,
c. 1880. On the grass
between the tents is
rustic cedar
furniture. Regarding
the use of tents in the
Adirondacks, see
figure 150*

65), a vindication for Stowe, a carpenter who lived alone in a cabin near Upper Saranac Lake.

In recent years writers and editors have referred to an "Adirondack style." Furniture in the Adirondack style often includes mosaic twig decoration or applied bark decoration, usually of white birch. Tables with polygonal tops and root bases or cagelike pedestals are characteristic pieces. In considering refinement as an attribute of Adirondack furniture, it is useful to remember that "mosaic twig work" requires the use of straight halved lengths of twigs hardly one-quarter inch in diameter. The use of larger rounds was common outside the Adirondacks, but these were coarser and the results might be better termed "rod work."

All of this furniture might generally be called "twiggy rustic," as it uses some recognizable part of the tree. Root, trunk, branch, twig, bark, pine cone, leaf—all have been employed, singly and in combination, in the making of this type of rustic art. Perhaps "tree art" better describes these objects. Whatever, it is furniture that retains some part of the tree, the real tree (or a mimicry of it in some other material), that constitutes the larger part of this book.

The second group of furniture to which the term "rustic" is applied in this book is cottage furniture; that which the landscape architect A. J. Downing (1815–1852) and his followers recommended for rural and country homes in America. To this furniture was added, between the 1890s and World War I, the squarish oak furniture advocated by Gustav Stickley (1848–1942) for the small suburban or vacation residence known as the bungalow. Rustic connotes country living, and it is in that popularly accepted sense that rustic furniture also finds a place in this book. Thus the hand-turned vernacular chair produced by Reuben Cary *(figure 304)* is rustic, as is the Craftsman-style furniture of the Swan family *(figure 267)* and Keene Valley Industries *(figure 273)*. The Westport chair *(figure 279)* is rustic, and so is its relative of uncertain parentage, the Adirondack chair *(figure 284)*. Chairs from Mottville, New York, common in Adirondack camps, perhaps come closest to Downing's notion of cottage furniture. Craftsman-style furniture, principally that of Gustav Stickley and his competitors (notably his brothers), is included even though it was made outside the Adirondacks. If it is known to have been used in the Adirondacks and stylistically belonged to those wood-lined, lairlike interiors that characterize the pre-1920 bungalow or cottage, then the furniture may be included here as rustic regardless of where it was made.

Why the interest in rustic things? Today, the city apartment may sport a rustic chair or bed as a respite from the monotonous lines and hard, artificial surfaces of machine-made furnishings. The Victorians would have regarded the use of twiggy rustic furniture in the parlor to be a dubious practice, but they would be very much in sympathy with the rest of the proposition, though perhaps with different emphasis. Accounts indicate that life in the city was no easier or more tolerable in 1850 or 1900 than it is today: too much confusion, hurry, indifference, hazard, pretense. These ills of urban life, it was believed, were due to people having removed themselves from Nature. If that sounds familiar, it should, since both problem and remedy, "getting away" to places like the Catskills or Adirondacks, remain unchanged except for such details as whether one travels by stagecoach, rail coach, or air coach.

Nature does not simply attract us with its beauties; it repels us with hostile spirits and creatures, symbols of the irrational or nonrational forces in ourselves. The deep forest in literature and the arts is a place of loss, trial, and salvation, an allegorical stage on which mankind wrestles with good and evil. Hence, our response to Nature goes far deeper than the pleasure of inhaling fresh air and watching a beautiful sunset. A rustic chair is a chair; it can be a key to the unconscious as well.

Rusticity is where you find it, in a vast forest preserve, in a city park, even in an apartment. Twig furniture in the city is a wish; in the Adirondacks years ago it confirmed the completion of the passage from polite society in the city to an informal, somewhat solitary life in the country. Simplicity and primitiveness, to the point of discomfort, were accepted as integral to a vacation in the woods, and the annual family summer retreat, which became an institution in America after the Civil War, resembled a religious pilgrimage. Creature comforts, such as auto campgrounds and cottages with hot water, a furnace, and a refrigerator, diminished the rigor of the vacation early in the century. Still, the wilderness seemed almost as real when viewed through the window of an Adirondack lodge as from within the small circle of light and warmth cast by a campfire in the woods.

Rustic is cunning, like Halloween masks and costumes, and the shudder it evokes is part real and part play. Branch, twig, and root are visible tokens of a domain outside human society. Just as Nature abhors a vacuum, so does it, at eye level at least, abhor the straight line and symmetry that are contrivances of the mind. Rustic is nonconformist, unpredictable, antic, ambiguous. Today's revival of interest in rustic work may be more than passing fancy, but rather a response under our technological skins to an age-old belief that trees really are occupied by gods or spirits. We may be druids at heart.

6

Printed notice from
Assembly Point,
a religious colony on
Lake George, 1890–
1900. Religion and
the sale of lots to
religiously minded
people underlay the
Assembly's brief
history

The Background: Rustic Taste in England and America

Chaise de bois brut.

Chaise.

Sopha de Jardin.

Chaise.

Table d'arbre brut.

Petit Fauteuil.

Canapé de treillage.

Chaise en branches.

Chaise.

Canapé.

Chaise.

Chaise.

Sopha dans le goût Chinois.

Chaise Chinoise.

Chaise. Chaise Gothique.

Sopha de tiges.

Chaise Gothique. Chaise.

Chaise. Table de Jardin.

Table Gothique. Chaise.

Canapé de tiges d'arbre brut.

Chaise. Dossier
pour des Bancs.

Dossier
pour des Bancs. Chaise.

Chaises de Jardin.

Chaise de Jardin.

Banc de repos de style Chinois

Chaise de Jardin.

Tree art, or objects fashioned from a recognizable part of the tree, came to the United States by way of England. "Rustic" generally was applied to trees, and the "rustic style" in the eighteenth century was merely one among a number of "tastes" that flourished for about forty years starting in the 1720s. Each had its leading motif: rococo its asymmetrical design, Gothic its gothic arch, chinoiserie its Chinese lattice-work, rustic its trunk and branch. All conjured up remote or exotic places and times, and are best understood when viewed as kindred variations on the picturesque, an aspect of Romanticism that had more to do with scenery and picture-making at this early stage than with profound emotion. The picturesque touched the visual arts with magical wit and whimsy, and it did much to humanize the century's formalism in the visual and decorative arts.

Twiggy rustic furniture and garden adornments only became widely popular in the first half of the nineteenth century, but designs for what clearly is tree furniture had begun to appear in Europe in the 1740s. The first English pattern book to include designs for rustic furniture was published in 1754, and its title, *A New Book of Chinese Designs*, suggests that the strong interest in chinoiserie in eighteenth-century England may have contributed to the development of rustic taste *(figure 9)*. The earliest use of twiggy rustic furniture in sophisticated settings occurred in China, where the tradition goes back hundreds of years *(figure 11)*. *Ideas for Rustic Furniture*, the first English design book entirely devoted to twiggy furniture, was published by 1780, and was still being reissued as late as 1835 *(figures 3 and 12)*. By the 1790s,

Johann Gottfried Grohmann's *Ideenmagazin*, a German periodical that contained an abundance of ideas for garden ornaments, including rustic furniture, was circulating throughout Europe *(figure 8)*.

Undoubtedly, one major impetus of rustic design in eighteenth-century England was the rise of the great landscape gardens with their picturesque garden architecture and furniture. Trees were used in these gardens not only as nursery stock but also for their dramatic appearance. The lengths to which landscape painter and architect William Kent (1684–1748) pursued these theatrical effects are related by Horace Walpole, especially his description of an episode in which Kent seriously considered planting dead trees in the garden at Kensington; the architect was "soon laughed out of this excess," says Walpole, who

10

A cottage in the northern Adirondacks incorporates the two decorative recesses with rustic ornamentation traditionally found in Japanese homes. The cottage was built by Japanese craftsmen who constructed a Japanese village at the 1901 Pan-American Exposition in Buffalo

11

Detail of a Chinese scroll called the Scholars of the Liu-Li Hall, *showing a man seated in a rustic chair. Thirteenth-century copy of a tenth-century painting by Chou Wen-chu*

nevertheless pointed out what he regarded as Kent's ruling principle: "Nature abhors a straight line." A variation of this observation was made by Sir Thomas Robinson, who noted that Kent's work on the garden at Carlton House was being done "without level or line." The agreeable result was gardens that possessed the "appearance of beautiful nature," yet were, for all their naturalness, as artificial as art itself.[1]

Ingenious terms were used to describe the ephemeral structures built for these gardens. The word "fabriques" referred to furniture and shelters which were taken down when their woodwork rotted and fashion tired of them. William Marshall called them "factitious accompaniments" in his 1786 book *On Planting and Rural Ornament*.[2] Summerhouses, prospect houses, gazebos, pavilions, belvederes: open on one or more sides, they nonetheless enclosed spaces and thus possessed an architectural character. Less so did such objects as benches, covered seats, fences, gates, arbors, and pergolas. Hermit's huts of logs, tree limbs, and straw were constructed in wooded areas of En-

Chairs

Designs for two rustic chairs, from Ideas for Rustic Furniture. *(London, c. 1780)*

glish parks to divert idle strollers. The grotto or cave was another type of hermitage associated with a hermit or a religious recluse. One of these, Merlin's Cave, was designed and built in 1735 by William Kent for Queen Caroline. A 1744 etching of the cave shows what may be the earliest example of rustic furniture in England *(figure 13)*.[3]

With the appetite for rustic design, there arose a trade to cater to it. As early as 1754, the cabinetmaker William Partridge advertised "Garden Seats, Window and Forrest Chairs and Stools," probably referring to rustic work. Robert Manwaring, a chair and cabinetmaker who de-

13

The Section of Merlin's Cave in the Royal Gardens at Richmond. *Etching by John Vardy, from* Some Designs of Inigo Jones and William Kent *(London, 1744)*

14

Rural Chairs for
Summer Houses,
*from Robert
Manwaring's* The
Cabinet and Chair-
Maker's Real Friend
and Companion
(London, 1765)

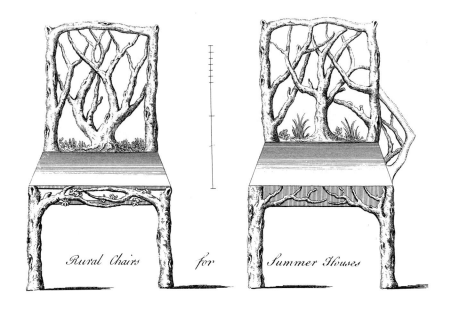

signed rustic furniture, stated: "I have made it my particular study to invent such Designs as may be easily executed by the hands of a tolerable skillful Workman."[1] A set of six chairs in the collection of the Victoria and Albert Museum closely resembles designs of two Manwaring chairs in his 1765 book *The Cabinet and Chair-Maker's Real Friend and Companion (figures 14 and 15)*. Too good to be exiled to a far corner of the garden yet not formal enough for the dining or public rooms of a main house, this set of chairs may have been intended for a conservatory, a banqueting building, or perhaps even a hunting lodge.

15

*Side chairs.
England, c. 1765.
Probably carved
beechwood, gessoed
and painted brown.
Victoria and Albert
Museum, London*

The eighteenth century was characterized by a concern for decorum. People and objects were given roles suitable to their station. When William Marshall described a hunting lodge in 1786, he stipulated that it should be masculine throughout, just as the breakfasting room of a principal residence should have "more masculine objects in view—wood, water and the extended countryside for the eye to wander over." Picturesque elements of the garden, particularly the twiggy kinds, belonged, like the stableboy, out of sight of the main house. Marshall felt that architectural ornaments were "embellishments" and should never be allowed to assume the character of "principals" unless placed "in a sequestered part of the extensive grounds."[5]

The nineteenth century was no less zealous about propriety as applied to art. Charles McIntosh invoked "taste and judgment" in the placement of garden furniture in his *Book of the Garden* (1853): "Rustic [twiggy] seats should be confined to rustic scenery, and the seats for a lawn, or highly-kept pleasure garden, ought to be of comparatively simple and architectural forms."[6] By "architectural" he meant dimensioned construction, such as framed benches. Rustic work, however, kept creeping ever closer to the Victorian house. McIntosh complained about frequent breaches of good taste, such as the "thatched summer-house placed in a flower-garden closely attached to the princely palace of Blenheim," which properly belonged, he felt, away from the mansion and its formal gardens.

Demand for garden furniture grew as English families of moderate wealth abandoned the city for the suburb and country. Villa gardens created a need for rustic work, and the twiggy kind was considered in harmony with the "English or natural style of laying out grounds."[7] Equally important, rustic ornament cost less than its architectural counterpart. Among the shops and small factories that arose to satisfy this need was that of T. Rutter, who called himself a "Summer House Builder"; he had been in business, according to his tradesman's card, since 1819 *(figures 16 and 17)*. It is easy to imagine Mr. Rutter taking out his pad of watercolor designs to show clients the rustic furniture and shelters he could fashion for their gardens.

Little is known about early rustic work and its makers. As McIntosh said, the craft was peculiarly tied to a special knack that had nothing to do with education or training: "It is next to useless to employ a carpenter [to manufacture rustic baskets, since] they work too much by square and rule, and, from habit, give their work too much the appearance of art." All rustic work was best done by "an intelligent labourer who has a natural [talent] for these things."[8] The time to do this was in winter, when workmen "can put together the material picked up from time to time during their usual occupations in the woods and forests . . . ," namely, "curious excrescences found on old trees, and the natural-bent branches."[9]

McIntosh went on to elaborate on the inimitable nature of rustic work, especially the mosaic kind, which called for split rods to be ap-

16, 17

Trade card of T. Rutter, who called himself a summer-house builder, London, c. 1825–50. The card is pasted into a pad of watercolor designs for rustic furniture and garden structures, including this one of a mosaic twig planter with a root base

plied in patterns to garden-house walls, tabletops, and benches: "It is a sort of natural taste that one man possesses which a thousand around him have not the slightest idea of. Hence it is that we have so few written instructions how these things are to be managed; and also because those who, for the most part, have excelled in this kind of work, have been unable to communicate even their ideas of it to paper, because they are in general men in the humblest walks of life. . . . Still we see nature has endowed even them with a peculiar gift that few educated men possess."[10]

The nineteenth century saw the proliferation of periodicals and popular books that dealt in an increasingly scientific way with gardening, indeed, with all aspects of plant and animal husbandry. These included pages filled with engravings, often accompanied by how-to explanations, a feature seldom found in eighteenth-century pattern books.[11] Among them was Shirley Hibberd's *Rustic Adornments for Homes of Taste* (1856), the most popular—and most lavishly illustrated—book of its kind. America was hardly less prolific than England in this regard, and the publishing output of both countries is evidence of the English-speaking world's passionate wooing of nature and its celebration of the benefits of the pastoral life.

Mosaic twig work was the nineteenth century's main contribution to rustic art. A correspondent in *The Gardener's Magazine* in 1834 wrote that the surfaces of outdoor shelters were being decorated with "wood mosaic," a treatment that he believed to be "rather a modern invention." The technique called for "split sticks of various lengths and sizes, and having bark of different colours" to be nailed to flat surfaces in elaborate patterns.[12] Adirondack craftsmen were to excel at this type of work.

Cast-iron furniture was another nineteenth-century innovation. The introduction of coke-processed iron, which ran more easily and could be poured into molds, made possible the fabrication of highly ornate furniture. A writer at mid-century observed, "Chairs in the rustic style, but of cast iron, appear to be becoming very prevalent."[13] One of the most imitated patterns, to judge from catalogues, was a vine-and-leaf design *(figures 18 and 19)*.

The most thorough technical exposition of rustic craft appeared in Paul Hasluck's *Rustic Carpentry* (1907), portions of which originally appeared as articles written by others in *Work*, a London periodical, between April 1889 and December 1891. The book, published in both England and America, was probably the first treatment of rustic carpentry as a subject in itself.

18, 19
Bench and chair.
New York City (?).
1850–1900. Cast
iron. Chair: The
Metropolitan
Museum of Art, New
York. Edgar J.
Kaufmann
Charitable
Foundation. Several
foundries produced
furniture like this
both before and after
the Civil War. A
similar bench
appears on the front
lawn of a country
inn in figure 285

Rustic work in America was not merely imitative of European precedents, nor was it solely an American invention. Europe's forested regions, from northern Italy through central Europe and into Scandinavia and northern Russia, had ancient traditions of timber construction that dated hundreds of years into the past. These vernacular expressions were transformed in the New World, where circumstances of climate and society produced scaled-down, temporary cabins and log houses that contrasted sharply with the larger, more elaborate wood domestic housing in settled districts of such places as Switzerland, Sweden, and Finland. When travelers thought of the new nation, they as often as not seized on the log cabin as a fitting symbol of America.

The *decorative* use of log construction, as opposed to its application for strictly utilitarian purposes, found early expression in America in the hermitage in Elias Hasket Derby's garden at his farm three miles from Salem, Massachusetts. The garden's two-story summerhouse designed by Samuel McIntire in 1793–94 still exists, but not this "little hut," built in 1793 and described by young Eliza Southgate, who visited the garden in 1802. Approaching the hut, which was sheltered by a weeping willow and "covered with bark," she lifted the latch of a small door that opened to reveal the carved figure of a "venerable old man" with a prayer book, seated at the old table.[14] The Derby hermitage is the earliest reference the author has found to tree art in America, and the garden itself, famous outside Massachusetts, came as close to English ideas about the landscape garden and the picturesque as anything in eighteenth-century America.

Rustic garden houses and furniture did not begin appearing in quantity in America until the 1840s. Their style was derived from theories and practices developed in Europe, principally England, during the last half of the eighteenth century. They were used, as in the English garden, to provide a visual accent with romantic connotations for the imagination, both as a compositional feature in the landscape to be seen from afar and as an invitation beckoning the stroller to a new vista yet to be enjoyed. They provided shelter from the sun and rain, and seats for relaxation and the contemplation of nature. An occasional rustic piece might become a symbolic relic. One such was the Charter Oak Chair *(figure 20)*, constructed in 1857 from the wood of the tree in which the royal charter guaranteeing the rights of self-government to Connecticut was believed to have been hidden in 1687 from the King's agents.

The popularity of rustic work in the United States was due as much or more to the publications of Andrew Jackson Downing as to any other person. Downing (1815–1852) interpreted English theory and practice

Charter Oak Chair.
Carved by John H.
Most, Hartford,
Connecticut, 1857.
Oak, height 61".
The Wadsworth
Atheneum, Hartford

of landscape gardening to American readers, and these he related to his own ideas about taste, domestic architecture, and furnishings for upper-middle-class American families, doing so in such books as *Cottage Residences* and *Treatise on the Theory and Practice of Landscape Gardening*, both of 1841, as well as in the periodical *The Horticulturist,* which he founded in 1846. He was an early advocate of public parks, and by the time of his early death at age thirty-seven, he had succeeded in consolidating ideas, galvanizing opinion, and establishing the beginnings of the profession of landscape design in America.

21

Rustic bench and shelter at the Newburgh estate of Andrew Jackson Downing, from a stereograph taken after Downing's death

Designs for rustic work appeared both in Downing's *Treatise* and in his periodical *The Horticulturist*. The latter was similar in format, content, and woodcut pictures to *The Gardener's Magazine*, which had been established in England in 1826 by John Claudius Loudon (1783–1843), and it is likely that Downing's ideas and illustrations were drawn to a degree from English precedents. Downing's four-acre home at Newburgh, New York, overlooking the Hudson, was said to have had, on its grounds, a hermitage and arbor constructed of rough logs with the bark on. A photograph taken after Downings' death purports to show a corner of his garden, with a rustic bench alongside a winding path and a summerhouse in the background *(figure 21)*. A vine-covered tower at the Mohonk Mountain House in the Shawangunk Mountains, just south of the Catskills, appears to be based on a design for "a rustic prospect tower" illustrated in Downing's *Treatise (figure 22)*. Mohonk's rustic architecture cannot have been built before the 1870s, but the date notwithstanding, the gardens and grounds encircling a lake, atop a mountain commanding dramatic views of the Hudson Valley and the

Catskill Mountains, are as near as one can get in America today to the spirit of the picturesque Victorian garden *(figure 2)*.

Illustrations of rustic work for the garden, porch, and even the home (although Downing had objected to rustic work in the hall) began to appear in such periodicals as *American Agriculturist* and *Illustrated Annual Register of Rural Affairs* during the 1850s. Shirley Hibberd's popular *Rustic Adornments for Homes of Taste* was pirated by Edward Sprague Read for a series of his own books, opening up a brief controversy between Hibberd and Read in the pages of *The Nation* in 1867. Books as well as periodicals carried advertisements in their back pages

22
Rustic tower,
Mohonk Mountain
House

for rustic baskets, birdhouses, garden furniture, and the like, from businesses which sold seeds, trees, and plants to farmers and gardeners.

Two landmarks of early American rustic architecture stand out. One was the "prospect arbor" erected between 1825 and 1830 in the twenty-three-acre garden that served as a nursery for André Parmentier in Brooklyn, New York. Parmentier, who came from a family of Belgian and French horticulturists, laid out gardens for estates along the Hudson River from 1824 until his death six years later. Downing regarded him as America's first and only practitioner of note in the emerging profession of landscape gardening, and recognized Parmentier's tower as "one of the finest pieces of rustic work of any size, and displaying any ingenuity."[15]

The other was Hornby Lodge, constructed in 1837–38 at the edge of a gorge high above the Genesee River, in western New York State. An octagonal building around a supporting giant oak tree, still retaining its bark, that poked through the center of the roof, the lodge incorporated tree limbs on its exterior and in the rooms. It was filled with furniture made from tree branches. Thomas Cole sketched the lodge in 1839 *(figure 23)*, and a description was published in 1845: "The ornaments of the lodge, over the doors and windows, and much of the furniture, are

Hornby Lodge, A Log Building Erected on a Romantic Spot Near the Falls of the Genesee. *Sketch by Thomas Cole, 1839*

. . . formed from the crookedest limbs of trees that could be found. [It stands] alone in its rustic beauty, . . . looking out fearfully upon the confined deep."[16] Hornby Lodge was designed and built by Elisha Johnson, a former mayor of Rochester and contractor who carved a tunnel out of the rock below the lodge as part of a scheme to build a canal around Portage Falls on the Genesee.

By the second quarter of the nineteenth century, rustic work began to appear in places of public assembly, highly social environments where Americans left the workaday world behind them. These ranged from city parks and seaside beaches, where people of all classes mingled for a day, to more remote spas for wealthy summer vacationers. They were diverse in their origin and purpose, but collectively they expressed the era's discovery of recreation and the importance of a healthful environment.

Many resort hotels, in the Adirondacks and elsewhere, had humble origins as cabins built by settlers whose land became more valuable for its scenery than its rocky soil. Eventually, the standard resort hotel appeared: typically a framed building painted white, three stories high and surrounded by columned porches on which guests could sit, chat, and take walks on hot or drizzily days. Old log houses often were preserved for guests who preferred the privacy of separate cottages. The first resort hotel in the Catskills was erected in 1823 on land that had been sought out by travelers for the majestic views it offered of the Hudson Valley to the east. Featured at the Mountain House was "the custom of bringing the outdoors within by lining the walls of public rooms with balsam-fir trees and boughs and sending spirals of hemlock and laurel climbing up pillars."[17] Rustic decoration was also used at other hotels before mid-century, but seldom as lavishly as at the Mountain House.

Religious campgrounds also took on a rustic air. An account of 1832 describes a camp where "rustic temples" had pews and pulpits "made of the rude timber just felled for the occasion." Rustic furniture was a part of the Methodist campground founded in 1835 on Martha's Vineyard. A Methodist resort on Wells Island in the Thousand Islands had a two-story log building with a shingle tower; both stories were enclosed by porches with railings and posts of slender tree trunks and branches.[18] Rural cemeteries, located on undeveloped tracts of land on the outskirts of cities but within a half hour's ride by carriage from the fashionable residential districts whose inhabitants they chiefly served, functioned as parks for the populace until the introduction of city parks at mid-century. Mount Auburn near Boston was the pioneer rural cemetery in America. Eleven years later, in 1842, Green-Wood Cemetery was established in Brooklyn, and it became a popular outing place. An early feature at Green-Wood was "a rustic cottage for the keeper, a rustic bell-tower, lodge and gate," constructed at the entrance in 1843 *(figure 24)*. This rustic enclave, closed in 1863 and later removed because it had deteriorated, was but one element of a larger picturesque landscape composed of lawns, trees, and flowering shrubs through which carriage drives and footpaths wound their way. The headstones and monuments—"sermons in stone"—served to remind the visitor of the brevity and unpredictability of life. Every Romantic cemetery had its examples of rustic art—common were tree trunks and limbs, often in the form of a cross, usually carved in marble, but also found in cast iron *(figure 25)*. Such cemeteries were "in reality parks and pleasure-gardens with, here and there, a monument or tombstone half seen among the trees,"[19] and they were the precursors of the city park in America.

24

Keeper's Lodge at Entrance of Green-Wood Cemetery, Brooklyn, N.Y. *Etching after a drawing by James Smillie, from* Green-Wood *(New York, 1847) by Nehemiah Cleaveland*

*Lloyd Family
Monument,
Hollywood Cemetery,
Richmond, Virginia.
J. H. Brown, c. 1895–
1900. The tree
represents strength
and mortality; the
climbing grapevine
alludes to faith and
fruitfulness; the
potted lily at the base
is a reminder of
Christian rebirth and
salvation*

A. J. Downing drew attention to the need for public parks in America's growing cities while space was still available, and he began to call for a park in New York City as early as 1848. His junior partner Calvert Vaux later became with Frederick Law Olmsted (1822–1903) a principal designer of Central Park, planned in 1857 as a "greensward" in what was then uptown Manhattan.[20]

The number of rustic structures in Central Park by the 1870s may never be known, but there must have been more than twenty; the display of rusticity was probably the most lavish anywhere *(figures 26 and 27)*. Much of it was of red cedar, cut in nearby Westchester County, and it set off a boomlet in rustic ornamentation elsewhere in the nation. An anonymous chronicler remarked in 1870, "The successful introduction of rustic work at the Park has done much towards popularizing it, for we now seldom visit a neighborhood where any attention is

With Summer lightnings of a Soul so full of Summer warmth, So glad, So healthy, Sound and clear and whole, his memory Scarce can make me Sad.

E. & H. T. ANTHONY & CO

591 BROADWAY, NEW YORK.

28

This shelter is the lone wood rustic survivor of the many that made New York's Central Park a force in the spread of rustic taste. Some rustic structures were razed in the 1930s, but Olmsted complained about poor maintenance of woodwork as early as 1872, suggesting that many of the original rustic features had probably disappeared by the end of the century

given to rural adornment that we do not see . . . attempts at this kind of decoration." Rustic carpentry was a collaborative endeavor between designer and builder. Vaux and his assistants, Jacob Wrey Mould and Julian Munckwitz, were architects, and Munckwitz was said to have designed a variety of pavilions in the park. Among the carpenter-builders, Anton Gerster, a Hungarian who, according to one observer, "showed a great aptitude for this kind of architecture,"[21] supervised the construction of many of the park's rustic structures. Prospect Park, begun in 1866 near Green-Wood Cemetery in Brooklyn, also incorporated rustic structures after plans drawn by Olmsted and Vaux.

Original outdoor rustic work was too vulnerable to weathering and mischief to survive the end of the nineteenth century. Olmsted and Vaux reported in 1872 that Central Park's "wooden foot bridges and woodwork generally are now in bad order, and partly from neglect of timely repair, much of their material will require to be replaced." Today a large cedar summerhouse, said by the Central Park Conservancy staff to be a nineteenth-century survivor, graces a section of the park known as the Ramble. It was joined in 1983 and 1985 by two more replicas: one in the Dene, near Fifth Avenue and Sixty-eighth Street, and one near the entrance at Central Park South and Sixth Avenue, called the Cop Cot *(figure 28)*.

Rustic work was also incorporated into the design of what was perhaps America's earliest suburban development, Llewellyn Park, in West Orange, New Jersey. The venture of L. S. Haskell, it was a conscious attempt to lure the well-off New York businessman and his family from their town house in the city to a mansion on three to five acres of lawn and trees in the country, all within an hour's ride from Wall Street. Among the attractions of Llewellyn Park were five hundred and fifty acres of land which had been set aside for six miles of shaded carriage roads, walks, pocket parks, and a rustic "wigwam" for the use of the eighteen families who by 1860 owned homes at the suburban park: "[It is] a curious and novel structure, furnished with rustic chairs and table in mosaic style. The roof is thatched with straw, and it is ornamented on top by the branches of a tree, much resembling the antlers of a deer."[22]

After the Civil War, as Americans became caught up in the race for wealth and possessions, a need for retreat from the world took hold among middle- and upper-class families. Americans began to build vacation homes in remote locales made newly accessible by an expanding network of railroads and highways, in places that architect Henry Hudson Holly in 1863 called "savage meccas for pale pilgrims."[23] Vacation havens away from the ocean appeared in the White and Green mountains of New England; the Adirondacks; the Upper Peninsula of Michigan and lake country of Minnesota; and the Rocky Mountains and Pacific Northwest. The American family thus discovered what sportsmen and writers like Thoreau had been saying for at least a generation, that one had to be active and self-reliant in the out-of-doors. Getting firewood was a necessity for the native, but an option for the summer visitor; still, the fire and satisfaction were as warm for one as for the other.

The establishment of state and national parks in the 1890s and early 1900s also gave an impetus to the design and construction of architecture in a rustic idiom. Old Faithful Inn at Yosemite, for example, was purposely planned to be in harmony with its natural surroundings. Constructed of logs, stone, and shingles, it was designed by Robert Reamer and erected in 1903–4 on land leased from the federal government. Photographs from the 1920s show that inside, Indiana hickory furniture was in conspicuous use. Another rustic-style hotel, El Tovar in Grand Canyon National Park, was designed by the architect Charles Whittlesey and built in 1905.

During the Depression of the 1930s the National Park Service employed teams of skilled architects, landscape designers, and administrators to plan and supervise the construction of park facilities. In addition, these experts were at the disposal of the state governments to help develop public parks as part of projects financed by the Works Progress Administration. A consistently high standard of design and construction was maintained in these projects, and the work was almost all in rustic styles. Thus the facilities were subordinate to their surroundings; construction materials were drawn from local trees, stones, and soil, and worked with the traditional skills of a given locality. Rustic furniture of peeled and mill-worked cedar was made for buildings in state parks in Arkansas and Texas. Even the Adirondack lean-to, identified as an "Adirondack shelter," found its place in the parks of other states.[24]

Boys and girls could learn outdoor skills at summer camps and scouting meetings—inventions of the 1880s and nineties and of the first decade of this century. For adults these things had to be learned pretty much by oneself, or so it seems, to judge by the volume of how-to articles and books written for tenderfoot readers that began appearing after the Civil War. Easily the most popular project was a log cabin: construction techniques and suggestions for furnishings were supplemented by floor plans, drawings, or photographs of interiors, and personal anecdotes encouraged the reader to leave his easy chair and build a hideaway in the woods. William S. Wicks, a charter member of the Adirondack League Club, who built a cottage on Honnedaga Lake in the western Adirondacks, wrote the most durable book on the subject in 1889, possibly the first to address the weekend hobbyist and seasonal builder.[25] Wicks, an architect, drew most of his illustrations after shelters and cottages in the Adirondacks (figure 38).

The celebrated nature writer John Burroughs (1837–1921) contributed to the log-cabin craze by closeting himself in Woodchuck Lodge, in Roxbury, New York, and recording his observations of the outdoors in popular books (figure 29). In 1895, he built another cabin, Slabsides, a few miles from his farm, Riverby. The cabin was framed, but sheathed outside with rough-barked slabs laid horizontally as though they were real logs. "A slab is the first cut from the log. I wanted to take a fresh cut of life—something that had the bark on."[26] Nearly seven thousand people, including tourists, journalists, and college students, some of them from Vassar College at Poughkeepsie on the other side of the river, visited Slabsides between the time it was completed and Burroughs's death nearly twenty-five years later.

"The house of logs appeals to us because it is part of our heredity," wrote Natale Curtis in 1911. "Today a house built of wood which has not been metamorphosed into board and shingle but still bears the semblance of the tree rouses in us the old instinctive feeling of kinship with the elemental world that is a natural heritage." Besides its primitive appeal and its association with such American heroes as Abraham Lincoln, a house of logs possessed "elements of intrinsic beauty. . . . There is the bare beauty of the logs themselves with their long lines and firm curves. Then there is the open charm of the structural features which are not hidden under plaster and ornament, but are clearly revealed." When Curtis recommends "orange hangings" and bookcases filled with books "to soften the crudity of the wood," we know that the world of Lincoln now reposes in the distant past.[27]

Another sign of change was a new vision of country life itself. "It is perfection, not simplicity, that must be our aim," wrote Bliss Carman, who reminded the readers of *The Craftsman* in June 1906 that, "It is useless to ask men of the twentieth century to live the life of the twelfth . . . We are more complex in our nature than the people of those times, and our life must be more complicated." Like the camel who gets his nose under the tent, the notion of *style*, in terms of both decor and daily life, was thus insinuated in the rustic camp. How should his reader occupy the months of June to November that Carman spent at his Ghost House in the Catskills? You would "have all the privacy of the wilderness, and yet all the essential luxuries of town," keeping "plenty of pleasant society . . . as soon as you had discovered that Thoreau didn't know everything after all. You would rise not too late, build a fire and make the bed, but a laundress would come and give the place a Christian cleaning as often as it needed it. After pottering around a bit, you would wander over to the nearby inn for breakfast, thanking your lucky stars that there was such a nice place to go to."[28] Carman is describing what he believes should be a *rustic style* of casual living, as distinctive as the Greek art and Japanese life to which he makes passing reference.

To help reconcile ideas about the simple life with the aspirations of the wealthy, *Country Life in America,* a large-format magazine founded in 1901, attempted to provide a credo for its readers. Among the purposes of the "Country Life Idea" were: "To draw people from the crowded cities, To foster a love for the wide outdoors, To encourage the owning of houses and land, To teach good taste in architecture and decoration."[29] By the first decade of the twentieth century, the camps going up on the shores of Adirondack lakes were hardly deficient in

29

John Burroughs at

Woodchuck Lodge

comfort and conveniences to the city apartment or the suburban house.

Each of the thousands of second homes being erected—cabin, cottage, or lodge—needed to be furnished. This was no small matter when there were living and dining rooms, kitchen and pantry, three or four bedrooms, a bath or two, a large porch, and a boathouse, along with extra rooms for guests or play to fill. There was, indeed, money in those hills, a fact not lost on *Country Life* or its advertisers.

Hickory furniture, produced at several shops in Indiana and sold by mail order as well as in department stores, was a convenient solution to the problem of furnishing a country retreat. Henry H. Saylor, an architect, expressed relief in 1911 that "camps, summer homes and cottages of similar character" could now be furnished, at least in part, with "the sort that is made of hickory. . . . How infinitely better this furniture is than the happily disappearing rustic sorts of the past generation."[30] Among his illustrations, which included houses from New England to California, was the Read Camp in the Adirondacks, designed by Augustus Shepard about 1907. On the porch was an assemblage of hickory furniture *(figure 30)* that may still be at the camp today. Woven furniture was also used, because wicker, rattan, and cane are natural, light, cool, and inexpensive *(figure 31)*. George Leland Hunter, a decorative-arts writer, recommended it in 1912 for its "gay vivacity" and "polite rusticity."[31]

30

*Porch of a lodge at
Read and Strange
Park, Tupper Lake,
New York, furnished
with Indiana hickory,
from Henry Saylor's*
Bungalows *(1911)*

31

Armchair. 1875–95.
Hardwood frame,
with rattan in a
chain-lock weave and
caning, height 41".
The Adirondack
Museum. Gift of
SUNY Cortland
Outdoor Education
Center.
The chair belonged to
William West
Durant at Camp
Pine Knot,
Raquette Lake, New
York

Attempts to promote the widespread use of branch and twig rustic furniture in vacation homes, however, got nowhere. The most conscientious advocate was *The Craftsman*, a periodical published by Gustav Stickley from 1901 to 1916 that found personal merit in the hobbyist who fabricated all kinds of things for the home. The magazine included measured diagrams for furniture that could be constructed with peeled poles and lumber by anyone with a few basic tools and a rudimentary knowledge of carpentry. But rustic work, except for Indiana hickory, was not susceptible to the quantity production that would have made it economic to market. The best rustic furniture was one-of-a-kind, and the best of that was made in the Adirondacks by men of talent, with no formal training except for the skills they had acquired while working as loggers and carpenters.

An Adirondack Aesthetic: From Shanty to Great Camp

32 (page 48)

Grandpa Cary. *Brandreth, Raquette, or Long lakes,*

c. 1895. Guide and carpenter Reuben Cary

(see page 319) plants his foot on the rustic chair at the left.

If a pipe was an attribute of the Adirondack guide,

it should be easy to tell natives from visitors

in this picture

33

Annex Interior to Ossahinta on 7th Lake.
This undated photograph of what appears
to be a hunting shanty captures the spirit
of a Hardy Boys adventure (their
fictional home was near Westport, in the
northeastern Adirondacks)

"An Adirondack camp does not mean a canvas tent or a bark wigwam," William Dix informed the readers of *The Independent* in July 1903. It was "a permanent home where the fortunate owners assemble for several weeks each year and live in perfect comfort and even luxury, though in the heart of the woods. . . ." Dix had come to the Adirondacks when these summer places were being built in a manner and in numbers sufficient to draw national attention. No two Adirondack camps were alike, he said: some were "elaborate, even to the point of questionable taste," some were "really summer cottages with all modern improvements, even to shaven lawns and formal flower beds," while others were "little more than shelter from the weather, with bunks furnished with balsam boughs." But the truest type, he concluded, was "composed of a group of rustic buildings on the edge of a lake, with pathless forests in the rear."[1]

"A camp in the Adirondacks may mean anything from a log fire in the woods to a hundred-thousand-dollar villa," Alice Kellogg wrote in *Broadway Magazine* in 1908. "The designation 'camp' has been stretched beyond its limits of meaning." She was favorably impressed, however, at finding "architectural perfection," which she attributed to "the artistic principle of suiting a design to its use and its situation."[2] Blame for this semantic confusion could be laid at the doorstep of Newport, Rhode Island, where seaside mansions were customarily called "cottages" by their owners. Dix and Kellogg merely reported what any traveler in the Adirondacks with a guide and suitable introductions could see with his own eyes—a hierarchy of woodland shelters, with the lean-to at the evolutionary bottom and the villagelike enclave of buildings that made up a great camp at the top. Uniting these structures was the forest and solitude, in which each and all, irrespective of size, were like tiny chips adrift on a real and metaphorical sea. The word "camp" contained a degree of false modesty and therefore of snobbishness; but while only those privileged with an invitation could know with any precision what the word meant when applied to a specific place, the term did possess the real virtue of implicitly acknowledging that nature was the center of attention and not the camp. Nature was the end and the camp the means for the enjoyment of the outdoors. So the term seems honest in its self-deprecation.

Vacation homes have always fallen outside the prescribed rules of taste. In the Adirondacks, the mannered cuteness of some names— Pine Knot and Kamp Kill Kare—together with inventions reminiscent of Indian names—Uncas, Minnewawa, Paowync (the initials of railroads in which the owner held stock!)—illustrates this suspension of judgment. Most regarded such lapses as innocent; others refused to be diverted. Raymond Spears, troubled at how the wilderness had been opened to private development, found woodlands that had "mysteriously slipped out of the public possession" and had been "turned into playgrounds for dilettantish people who built huge mansions and called them 'camps,' who graveled walks through the woods and called them 'trails,' and who put gorgeous little open yachts on the lakes and called them 'skiffs.' " He deplored the demands these camps made on public services: alluding to a forest fire that menaced Camp Nahasane, he said that "hundreds of firefighters [were] necessary to save the great 'camp.' "[3] His quotation marks reminded readers that the camp he referred to amounted to a good deal more than a crude building or two. Today "great camp" distinguishes one with multiple buildings from camps consisting of a cottage and perhaps a boathouse.

Large Adirondack camps gave a new meaning to "roughing it." A newspaper cartoon of 1926 showed President Coolidge seated alone in a rowboat on Osgood Pond, the twenty-six buildings of White Pine Camp behind him. He says to himself, "Everything to delight a New England president of simple habits" *(figure 34)*. This camp, constructed of the rough-sawn planking with uneven edges known as "brainstorm" siding, included two greenhouses, tennis courts, and a bowling alley, not to mention a Japanese teahouse pagoda.

34

Roughing It, *cartoon by Will R. Johnstone and Robert Barry for* The New York World *in the summer of 1926. White Pine Camp belonged to the publisher of the* Kansas City Star.

Most Adirondack camps came by their rustic style and character by heritage, since the materials of rustic construction and decoration originated in the strictly utilitarian or subsistence buildings that were still being erected in the region, principally for logging camps, until the Depression. Logs for walls and sheets of bark for the roof, readily at hand, stimulated subsequent variations for a generation largely ignorant about survival skills in the woods. Adirondack carpenters, fresh from the forest, placed bark on ceilings and around fireplaces; they cut three-inch saplings when the sap was down in winter and fashioned them into stair and porch railings of unbarked spruce, cedar, and yellow birch rounds. Or they split the saplings and applied them flat side down in herringbone or some other pattern in the triangular spaces below the roof peak, at the gable ends of cottages. The rustic materials and techniques were their own, although interest in natural materials and the effects of color, texture, and mass very much belonged to the medley of domestic styles of the period between the Civil War and World War I.

Principal among the modest rustic structures built throughout the Adirondacks was the house of hewn logs, usually a story-and-a-half high, with two floors. An example is Tyler Merwin's log house, part of his hotel, the Blue Mountain House, which became the site of the Adirondack Museum in 1955 *(figure 35)*. Related to the log house was its poorer cousin, the log cabin, with a single floor and one room, which was sometimes partitioned according to the owner's whim. "Shanty" was the term commonly used by travelers in the Adirondacks for log cabin, but it could also mean an enclosed bark shelter or lean-to. The art of building bark shelters may have originated with the Indians, but in general the primitive log cabin, shanty, and lean-to were less representative of a vernacular *tradition* of construction than they were embodiments of the adage that necessity is the mother of invention. Noah John Rondeau's hut and furniture probably belong in this category *(figures 36 and 88)*. Early basic structures shared at least two features: they were constructed from local materials and their sole purpose was to provide shelter.

In 1841, minister John Todd, arriving at the head of Long Lake, found "a little community of eight or nine families" shut off from the world, living in "little log-houses," one being "covered with hemlock bark," possibly a reference to barked logs forming the walls or to bark sheets covering the roof. By 1880, J. P. Lundy, a dyspeptic minister from Philadelphia convalescing at Saranac Lake, noticed that there were "about fifty or sixty log and frame houses."[4]

Adirondack homes located near good hunting and fishing country were often turned into hotels. Dr. Arpad Gerster, on a trout-fishing trip with his son in August 1898, stayed the night at Mrs. Kenwell's hotel on Moose River: "The place is the genuine old fashioned primitive Adirondack 'place,' with home-made furniture, unplaned boards for ceiling, walls and floors, and peeled rough rafters supporting things overhead. In the 'parlor' [are] a few rickety chairs, a stove and organ." The surgeon watched Mrs. Kenwell at work in the kitchen from his seat in the dining room, "the good housewife having no reasons to hide any of the mysteries of her art."[5] Dr. Gerster's diary in the Adirondack Museum library is one of the most pungent documents about summer life in the Adirondacks.

A similarly authentic log house with an attached shed that stood in a clearing overlooking the Cedar River in the vicinity of Indian Lake was described by a teenage girl in 1859. Outside the logs retained their bark, which meant they were still round; but they had been hewn flat

35

Log Hotel of Blue

Mountain House,

built in 1876

36

Noah John Rondeau's log hut, Cold River country, c. 1935–50, as exhibited at the Adirondack Museum. The lifesize sculpture of Rondeau was carved from Michigan pine in 1977–78 by Robert Longhurst, Crown Point, New York

inside the house and the spaces between filled with plaster or cement, so "there is alternately a light and dark stripe." On the ground floor of the story and a half house were a parlor, dining room with pantry, and two bedrooms. Above, reached by a steep flight of stairs, was the garret, which the sprightly girl called "one large dormitory in which are seven beds," a hint that the house had been adapted to a more public role. A shed for the kitchen was attached to the dining room and pantry.

The house was furnished simply. The parlor contained a stove, barrels and boxes, benches, satchels, and chairs, with "hangings of shawls, bonnets and coats, and other things too numerous to mention." The large bedroom faced the river and had a window and door to the outside, commanding "lovely views of river and mountains, and two large trees, all alive with birds flitting in and out in the most entertaining manner." The bedsteads were all made of the same board material as the white-painted partitions that separated the rooms. And of the mattresses, the narrator writes: "I never slept more sweetly than I do on my bed of straw."[6]

The true shanty cannot be reduced to a single structural type: it was a subsistence dwelling that usually employed logs but, true to its opportunistic character, might utilize anything scavenged in the neighborhood. Guides, trappers, hunters on the prowl were grateful for a shanty, since it was generally dry and often had a small fireplace or stove for cooking and warmth. It is distinguished from the log cabin by its small size and ramshackle appearance; three men in wet clothes was a crowd in a shanty, but disrepair and tight quarters were tolerable when nights turned cold and rain pounded the roof. One writer described a shanty he had found a short distance from Chateaugay Lake, surrounded by trees: "It is a rough log hut, boasting of one room [furnished with] an unplaned plank table, a couple of logs flattened on one side . . . which bore the dignified title of stools, and an ancient looking cooking stove with its pipe sticking out of a wood chimney in the roof."[7]

Most log shanties were used seasonally, by trappers in winter and by trapper guides and their sportsmen patrons in summer and fall. A few, such as Billy Wood's on Raquette Lake in the 1840s, were occupied year-round. Wood's camp was of log construction and had a "bark-covered porch in front." Shanties were "rustic" by nature, unlike hewn-log houses which could always be socially upgraded by adding clapboards and paint. Several simple bark shanties were encountered by artist Jervis McEntee during a trip that brought him to Billy Wood's home in the 1840s *(figure 37)*.

"Here we shantied," wrote a college student from Rome, New York, speaking of one of a number of woodland shelters that his guide scouted up in the course of a three-week camping trip from Lowville to Newcomb in July 1853: "We found a little way up stream the best log shanty

37

Wood's Cabin on Rackett Lake, July 1851. *Pencil drawing from the sketchbook of Jervis McEntee (1829–91). Wood lost both legs below the knee one winter but still managed to keep a garden and put up sportsmen like artist Jervis McEntee*

AN ADIRONDACK
AESTHETIC:
FROM SHANTY TO
GREAT CAMP

56

fortune had thrown our way. Its roof is low but snug and tight. It is probably fourteen-by-twelve-feet large. . . . The cabin is of hewn hemlock logs with a large ridge beam for the roof, which is highest in the center like that of an ordinary house. The room has no windows or flooring, & for beds fresh boughs have been strewn around."[8]

In logging camps were found the largest versions of the shanty. Constructed from whole logs with bark roofs, these one-story structures were either abandoned in the woods or dismantled and moved by teams of men and horses to another district with fresh stands of timber. Such was Rousseau Shanty, "an old landmark" described by Arpad Gerster as "an untidy, spidery, brokendown, abandoned lumber shanty."

The simplest shelter of all, called an open camp by Adirondack guides and a lean-to by summer residents, became, like the Adirondack guideboat, a symbol of the pleasures and healthy rigors of roaming the wilds and living off nature's storehouse *(figure 39)*. The lean-to was open on one side. It had a sloping back wall of overlapping sheets of bark laid on a grid of saplings which touched the ground at the rear and were supported in the front, approximately at eye level, by a horizontal pole

38

Interior of Cabin in Adirondacks, *from* Log Cabins and Cottages *by William S. Wicks. The book, published in 1889, was more an inspiration than a practical treatise for those headed for the frontier. The author, who belonged to the Adirondack League Club, illustrated actual examples, the majority of which had an Adirondack locale*

Camp Colden.
Photograph by
George B. Wood,
1886. Two sportsmen
sit at a table of birch
poles in front of a
bark-covered lean-to,
while their guides
prepare food

40
Andrew Fisher, a
guide and carpenter
who made rustic
furniture (see figure
209), at Endion,
Long Lake, New
York, 1900–10.
Fisher is standing in
front of a substantial
open camp, whose
eaves are trimmed
with evergreen
boughs

on which the saplings rested; the ends of the pole itself rested in the crotches of two trees or saplings that had been cut and stuck into the ground. The lean-to kept occupants dry from all except a driving rain; a giant log or stone in front reflected heat (and smoke) into this most primitive of man-made shelters in the woods. Many lean-tos were placed so as to afford a view of a lake or rushing brook or, in the high peaks region of the Adirondacks to the east, of a range of mountains framed by giant pine or hemlock trees.

If the sapling and bark shelter embodied the Adirondack experience at its most footloose, then its offspring of logs, lumber, and shingles marked the arrival of the domesticated version *(figure 40)*. Every self-respecting camp owner had one or more open camps on his property, usually near the lakefront and as far from the lodge as possible. The tender ends of evergreen boughs—balsam and hemlock—were bundled and laid stick-end downward on the platform to form a fragrant, soft cushion or mattress.

Adirondack men often possessed the skills of the guide, the logger, and the carpenter. "My occupation," said Seth Pierce, "is guiding, fishing and hunting, and once in a while I take my tools and go at carpenter work."[9] It was from this pool of skilled and semiskilled labor that William West Durant and others built a resort empire. "James B. Rexford, G. H. Rogers, Joshua Smith and Charles Dougherty left [North Creek] Monday for Newcomb, where they will be employed at carpenter work on W. W. Durant's camps." Area newspapers, such as the *Lake George–Warrenburg News* for February 2, 1899, were full of employment gossip during the boom in camp construction, from about 1880 to 1930.

During the heyday of camp construction in the Adirondacks, perhaps thirty architects designed camps and other rustic structures. Nearly all of them had offices elsewhere, often in New York City. Only Augustus D. Shepard made a national reputation for his Adirondack work, and camp architecture never achieved real visibility and respectability in the profession. Some of these architects deserve recognition for their contribution to a unique rustic style. Of course, there are also ambitious and original buildings in the Adirondacks to which no architect's name can be attached. One example is the Adirondack Lodge, built in 1878–79 on Clear (now Heart) Lake, and destroyed by fire in 1903. This large log building had a porch whose roof was supported by twenty-one posts with rustic capitals, each one an inverted stump placed atop the trunk of a spruce tree *(figure 41)*.

WILLIAM WEST DURANT (1850–1934): What Durant brought to the Adirondacks was a cultivated eye and his father's instinct for seizing an opportunity and pursuing it to personal advantage.[10] Educated privately and at Twickenham School in England, he traveled widely in Europe with his mother, sister, and a cousin, returning to the United States only once or twice between 1861 and 1873. (Alexander Pope's home, with a picturesque garden that included rustic elements, was located in Twickenham, but any influence it may have exerted on young Durant is conjectural.) His father, Dr. Thomas Clark Durant, practiced medicine for several years before he turned to railroading in the American West. It was through his father's contacts that Durant easily won entree to the houses of many prominent families in New York society and to the offices of the city's men of business and politics. His tastes and proclivities, conditioned by years as the "man of the family" while his father built the Union Pacific Railroad, were those of a socialite. He possessed a capacity for sustained work whether in a city office or in the Adirondack wilds. Sent to the Adirondacks by his father at the age of twenty-five, Durant assisted in putting together a family empire that would sell land, timber, and minerals, control the transportation of goods and tourists on railroads, stages, and steamboats, and build or otherwise encourage the construction of hotels, camps, and clubs.

After his father's death in 1885 and the sale of the family's Saratoga–North Creek railroad in 1889, Durant turned to the speculative construction of what later would be called great camps, which he intended to sell to a wealthy clientele. He assembled teams of workers and servants, and by using their native skills and intelligence, he showed them how to build and serve in a style that was refined and rustic at the same time. This "school" of employees continued to exert Durant's influence long after his bankruptcy and departure from the Adirondacks in 1903–4. His camps were inspected by potential owners and their architects, and they served as exemplary models of what could be achieved with indigenous materials and discriminating taste.

Camp Pine Knot was the first of the four great camps that Durant built in the last quarter of the nineteenth century. Pine Knot, started in 1876–77, was sold to railroad tycoon Collis P. Huntington in 1895. Camp Uncas followed; built in 1893–95, it was sold on completion to banker J. Pierpont Morgan. Sagamore Lodge was constructed in 1897–1901 and then sold to young Alfred G. Vanderbilt, who had inherited a $36-million railroad fortune in 1898. Arbutus Camp, completed in 1898–99, was purchased by Collis P. Huntington for his adopted son, Archer. Except for Arbutus, these great camps, characterized by their many

41
Adirondack Lodge.
Photograph by
Seneca Ray
Stoddard, 1888

42
William West
Durant (right), with
his father and his
wife of four months.
Saratoga, New York,
1885

cottages and service buildings on large tracts of land, are in a fair state of preservation today, retaining much from the Durant era as well as additions by later owners.

Pine Knot was not built in a piece, but rather grew in stages. Seneca Ray Stoddard, a late-nineteenth-century photographer and publisher of an annual travelers' guide to the Adirondacks, observed that camps like Pine Knot were "never completed *really*," being "bound by no rule of time or architecture" and "never exactly the same one year [as] the year before." The camp was sufficiently developed in 1881 for Stoddard to call it "unquestionably the most picturesque and *recherché* affair of its kind in the wilderness." Seven years later there were enough camps on Raquette Lake and its environs, most of them owned by the Durant family or their friends, for Stoddard to discern the influence of an emerging rustic aesthetic. "The camps of Raquette Lake are elegant affairs, and although built of rustic material found ready at hand, it is apparent that twisted cedar, shaggy spruce and silvery birch, in their native vestments, were not chosen because they cost nothing there. Some of these camps are works of art, [generally] pertaining to woodsy things, and in keeping with their native environment. The pioneer camp of this section, and one of the most artistic in the woods, is Camp Pine Knot on the South Bay." [11] Thirty years later Alfred L. Donaldson, whose history of the Adirondacks has not been supplanted, said of Pine Knot: "Before [it] was built there was nothing like it. Since then, despite infinite variations, there has been nothing essentially different from it." [12]

44

Camp Pine Knot,

Raquette Lake.

Photograph by

Edward Bierstadt,

c. 1885

Durant later remarked on his first visit to Raquette Lake in the summer of 1876, when he saw the guide and trapper Alvah Dunning's camp on Osprey Island, "As I recollect it, it was a low roofed camp; I had never seen anything like it in this country before, or any kind of country like this: . . . there was some bark on it and I think some boards."[13] His rustic aesthetic owed something to the rough-and-ready shanties that had been built by two to three generations of men like Dunning.

What Durant did at Pine Knot was dress up the cottage exteriors with spruce and cedar bark applied to exterior walls of boards or planking and around windows and on the front of doors *(figure 43)*. He applied bark to the roof of the outdoor dining pavilion as well, though this was eventually replaced by cedar shingles. By the 1890s exterior materials included white-birch bark with twig trim on the large bay window of the recreation building, an experiment not taken up elsewhere. In addition, he used bark-covered cedar posts for the railings and balustrades of steps and porches. These rustic accents were set off by connecting paths. Lanterns were placed along them, and planters made from hollowed-out stumps in which flowers such as nasturtiums grew. The Swiss Cottage, focal point of the camp, was partially obscured behind a broad-leafed vine that grew luxuriantly up railings and posts to the porches on the upper floor. Guests conveyed back across Raquette Lake in the deepening night could take their bearings from a bonfire lighted for their departure and colored lanterns strung up along Pine Knot's shoreline.[14]

45

Camp Cedars,

Forked Lake.

Photograph by

Edward Bierstadt,

c. 1885

The interiors of Camp Pine Knot's first cottages, built in the 1870s, were unfinished: hewn-log walls chinked with plaster or cement remained exposed or, next to beds, partly covered by heavy fabric or paper (see *figure 45* for a similar example at Camp Cedars). Eventually these walls were concealed behind wainscoting—first, narrow beaded boards laid vertically, and then wider, beveled boards laid horizontally to resemble the inside face of hewn logs. Durant used the latter device at Camp Uncas *(figure 151)* and Sagamore Lodge, and it would turn up again at camps elsewhere in the Adirondacks, notably at Kamp Kill Kare *(figures 125 and 139)*. The stovepipes conspicuous in early photographs were soon replaced with stone and brick chimneys; a stickler for fine stone- and brickwork, Durant personally saw to it that fireplaces, hearths, and chimneys were laid strictly to plan, usually his own or one approved by him *(figure 162 and plate 5)*. He once ordered a stonemason to take down part of a fireplace because one stone in it did not match the others.

An innovation found at Camp Pine Knot, as well as Camps Cedars and (possibly) Fairview, built for Durant's nephews between 1876 and 1885, was the use of unbarked cedar posts and sheets of cedar bark and white birch bark as decoration around the fireplaces and on chimney breasts above the mantel. The fire hazard, along with a change in taste, no doubt explains why this practice was discontinued by about 1890. But rather than give up bark altogether, Durant placed sheets of birch bark between the peeled-pole rafters that supported the roof. Ceilings open to the rafters had presented a problem of finishing: oil paper and rough-woven fabric had been used to cover unsightly roof planking, but birch bark, readily available in the woods nearby, was far more satisfactory and cheaper besides. It also helped brighten interiors made gloomy by the fashionably dark-stained walls and by the shade of the spruce, hemlock, and pine trees that soared high above most camp cottages. Birch continued to be used in this way by architects William Coulter and William Distin *(figure 49)*, both of whom knew Durant's camps and the standard these established for an acclaimed rustic aesthetic.

The amount of rustic furniture varied from camp to camp. Camps on Raquette Lake and its vicinity, where more rustic furniture and camps were built than anywhere else in the Adirondacks, each contained a dozen or so examples during the early decades of camp construction from the 1870s to the nineties. The inventory for Pine Knot that William West Durant turned over to Collis P. Huntington when the property was sold in 1895 used the word "rustic" in connection with only twenty-four items. This represented nearly thirty years of accumulation at the camp: the conclusion, which is supported by historic photographs of camp interiors, is that rustic furniture was used sparingly but that it enhanced the regional flavor of Adirondack interiors where factory-made cottage furniture generally prevailed *(figures 162 and 237)*.

WILLIAM L. COULTER (c.1865–1907): By 1904, peeled-pole furniture of the kind that Durant introduced at Camp Uncas in 1895 and Sagamore Lodge in 1899 *(figure 151 and plate 1)* was being installed in the Lower Saranac Lake camp that William L. Coulter designed for Adolf Lewisohn. Coulter was a New York architect who moved to Saranac Lake in 1897 for his health; almost certainly he saw Durant's Sagamore Lodge in 1901, when the lodge's new owner, Alfred G. Vanderbilt, wanted to add a recreation building to the site and asked Coulter to design it.

The architectural firm that Coulter founded at Saranac Lake in about 1897, which survived his death in 1907, specialized in designing Adirondack great camps.[15] Among his credits, and those of his junior partner, Max Westhoff, were compounds for Governor Levi Morton, Adolf Lewisohn, and Otto Kahn, and for the group of relatives and friends who commissioned eight buildings at the Knollwood Club *(figures 47 and 49)*. Coulter employed William G. Distin, who worked with him and Westhoff for about five years before entering Columbia University,

46

William L. Coulter,
Saranac Lake, New
York, 1896

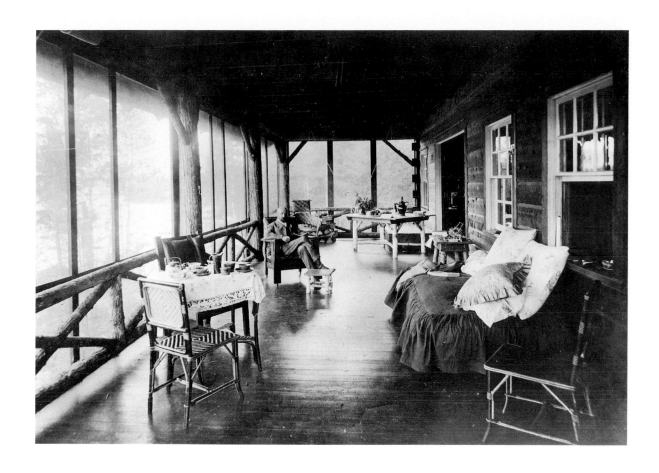

47

Screened porch,

possibly Knollwood.

Lower Saranac Lake,

c. 1900–5. William

L. Coulter, who

designed eight

buildings for

Knollwood, may be

the man seated in the

Craftsman-style

chair. At the far end

of the porch a locally

made rustic table

and an Indiana

hickory chair can

be seen

where he received his architecture degree in 1910. Distin rejoined the firm about 1915 and within a few years the practice was in his name. He designed about twenty Adirondack camps and cottages, the last being Camp Minnowbrook, built on Blue Mountain Lake in 1948–49. Distin carried on the tradition of rustic architecture that Durant had introduced and established from 1876 to 1901 and Coulter had practiced from 1897 to 1907 *(See plates 22, 26, and 27).*

Distin acknowledged Coulter's influence: "His work in this area was principally large Adirondack camps and lodges upon which I worked with him in design, detailing and supervision, and where I had my early training in this unique field." He credited Durant with pioneering the type of rustic camp on which his firm had earned its reputation.[16] Durant's influence, principally through Coulter, reached beyond the Raquette Lake region to the large camps that the firm would construct near Saranac Lake, some forty miles farther north.

ROBERT H. ROBERTSON (1849–1919): A watercolorist who traveled the Adirondack wilds extensively as well as an architect, Robertson designed two notable Adirondack camps: Nahasane and Santanoni. He

came from a Philadelphia family whose ties to the Adirondacks dated back to at least the 1850s, but his office and home were in New York City.

For William Seward Webb, who was the driving force behind the first railroad across the Adirondacks, Robertson designed in 1890–91 a sprawling lodge in shingle or free-classic style. Nahasane overlooked an expanse of green lawn sloping to the edge of Lake Lila, named for Webb's wife, the former Lila Vanderbilt. Architecturally impressive on the outside, Nahasane was less so inside except for the living room, with its timbered cathedral ceiling and massive stone fireplace. New York State, following a policy of adding to its holdings in the Adirondacks, purchased nearly 15,000 acres of land from the Webb family and estate in 1978. Once it became part of the State Forest Preserve, the lodge and other nonconforming buildings were doomed for demolition, which took place in 1983. More than half of Nahasane Park's pre-1978 acreage remains in private hands.

More original and important was Camp Santanoni, which Robertson designed for the Pruyn family of Albany at about the same time he was planning the Webb lodge. Its five cottages, constructed from peeled and varnished logs, were connected to one another by a vast, roofed-over veranda covering some 5,000 square feet, whose frontage alone measured 265 feet. So far as the author knows, there was never a structure like it anywhere in the Adirondacks *(figure 50)*. The interiors of Santanoni were rustic, its walls and ceilings covered with sheets of birch bark, and stair railings, window casings, and wainscoting made from hardwood and unbarked cedar sticks. In 1972, the 12,500-acre preserve was sold to New York State. The main camp itself, set back from Newcomb Lake, is locked and boarded up, though its exterior can be seen by those willing to walk five miles up a road from the highway at Newcomb. The interiors at Santanoni, now empty, once contained what one state employee said was a "considerable amount" of rustic furniture.

AUGUSTUS D. SHEPARD (c.1869–1955): The equal of Coulter and Distin in the quality and body of his architectural work, Shepard was a partner in the New York City firm of Davis, McGrath and Shepard. Like Robertson's, his family had early ties to the Adirondacks. "As a boy," wrote one friend, "Mr. Shepard roamed the Adirondacks and acquired

49

Living room of one of six cottages built in 1900 at the Knollwood Club, Lower Saranac Lake, 1900–5

an early and zealous affection for their rough wild beauty."[17] In his early twenties, about 1891, Shepard became a member of the Adirondack League Club, and the club, which owned some 100,000 acres of land south of Old Forge, New York, later provided Shepard's chief patronage. Between the late 1890s and the early 1930s, he designed several clubhouses and as many as twenty-five camps for the club and its members, principally on Little Moose Lake, as well as the Read Camp for William Read on Lake Wilburt (now Little Simon Pond) *(figure 30)*.

Shepard graduated from the Lawrenceville School in Lawrenceville, New Jersey, in 1889 and then studied architecture in the United States and Europe. He was best known for his mountain lodges and country estates. He considered stone fireplaces his specialty, and he also designed rustic furniture, wall brackets, and chandeliers fashioned from peeled-pole work and wrought iron.

Shepard's camps were both sophisticated and practical. He peeled the bark from spruce or pine logs and removed idiosyncrasies from rustic trim. Trophies, usually deer heads, conspicuous at earlier camps, were few, for in their furnishings and landscaping—including an occasional flagstone terrace surrounded by clipped lawns—the spirit of Shepard's estates was closer to the businessman who had turned matters over to his wife's decorator than to the rough-and-ready sportsman's camp of old *(figure 51)*.

50
Santanoni Lodge, Newcomb Lake, New York, in 1975

At the same time Shepard, more successfully than any other architect in the Adirondacks, achieved his goal of designing camp buildings "so that one feels no change in environment in going from the woods into a camp."[18] His exteriors and interiors were happily integrated with their surroundings, and he placed great emphasis on the contours of each site. His plans fell into three groups. The "boathouse camp" was used for sites that dropped abruptly toward a lake: centered on a two-story boathouse with a living room and deck above, two one-story wings branched out in this plan forming a "V," with the kitchen, dining room, and servants' quarters in one wing and the master bedrooms in the other. Just beyond the bedroom wing were cottages or tents for guests. He used the second type, the "separate boathouse camp," for sites with more gradual slopes: it also called for a V-shaped building, the two wings joining at the living room. (William Distin followed a similar layout, on a grander scale, at Wonundra, designed for William Rockefeller on Upper Saranac Lake about 1932.) The "separate building camp," the third plan, was determined less by the terrain than by the owner's desire for privacy. This plan, of detached buildings, was not original to Shepard's camps; most of the great camps, including the first, William West Durant's Camp Pine Knot, adopted it. Shepard imposed considerable control over the arrangement of buildings, and

51

A corner of the living room of a private camp at the Adirondack League Club, showing peeled poles for decoration and peeled logs for construction, from Augustus D. Shepard's Camps of the Woods *(1931)*

he paid greater attention to landscaping with lawn and shrubs. This allowed sun to reach the buildings and fill the interiors with cheerful light. Site selection and landscape design were not done elsewhere with anything like the care that Shepard brought to camp construction. Unlike the majority of architects who designed buildings in the Adirondacks, Shepard was thoroughly familiar with his building sites, since most of his commissions were on Adirondack League Club property where he lived and worked.

Shepard's preference for integrating buildings with environment suggested low structures. The privacy lost by lining up the bedrooms was mitigated by doors in each that opened directly to the terrace or lawn. Because a building was rarely more than one room deep, most rooms had views in two directions and were flooded with daylight. Shepard incorporated large areas of glass into his camps, using picture windows freely; he was especially fond of French doors and windows with glass panes that reached nearly from floor to cornice.

His living and dining rooms were airy, generally open to the roof, where peeled-pole rafters, trusses, and posts exemplified his kind of rusticity. Floors might be stained dark, but the woodwork, both pole work and paneling, was left in its original light color *(plate 50)*. The dark interiors of the Arts and Crafts era, like protective lairs, had yielded to the professional eye of the architect and interior decorator. Shepard's interiors have something of the Colonial Revival in their subordination of parts to an overall effect, attenuated and muted. This was not a failing, since to neutralize the interior was one way—perhaps the best way—of diverting attention to the natural environment that surrounded each camp.

In the brief span of fifty years, Adirondack rustic, which once would have described the shanty that Alvah Dunning called "hum," came to suggest such grandly appointed estates as Kamp Kill Kare of the Woodruffs, its floors and walls covered with animal skins, stuffed birds, and deer trophies, together with steel traps, knives, rifles, and "other implements of the chase" *(figure 125)*.[19] The appreciation of nature that gradually replaced these atavistic symbols of predation in the twentieth century was more sensitive, though not more intense or joyous, than when men roamed the woods unhampered by possessions and worries other than those of the moment.

Plate 1

Living room, Manor House, Camp Uncas, c. 1893–95. The open-floor plan at Camp Uncas was so far ahead of Durant's earlier Camp Pine Knot that one suspects the design was by a professional architect

Plate 2
Filigree rustic work
fills a gable built
over the porch of the
Recreation Building
at Camp Pine Knot.
A second gable above
this one has a solid
sunburst pattern

Plate 3

An idealized

Adirondack interior,

as installed at the

Adirondack Museum

by William Vernor

and Edward

Comstock, Jr.,

1977–78

Plate 4
The Adirondack
Cottage, installation
at the Adirondack
Museum. Before
the Blue Mountain
House became a
museum in 1957,
the cottage housed
guests of the hotel.
The American
Impressionist
painter Gustav
Wiegand used the
cottage as a summer
studio in c. 1910–20,
hence the skylight.
The bed is cedar. See
figure 118 and plate
39 for the stand and
showcase

Plate 5

*Living room, Durant
Cottage, Camp Pine
Knot, c. 1890. Note
the unusual niches in
the mantel above the
stone fireplace. See
figure 99 for the
chair. A companion
of the bed appears in
figure 103*

Plate 8

Living room, Camp Topridge. The rustic furniture and
horn chandeliers were made locally. The room once had
far more furnishings than this recent photograph shows:
many of Mrs. Post's artifacts went to the Smithsonian
Institution after her death in 1974

Adirondack Tree Furniture

52 (page 80)
*Brandreth family
members on the
porch at Trophy
Lodge, posing in
front of a sideboard
decorated with
mosaic twig work
(see figure 206)*

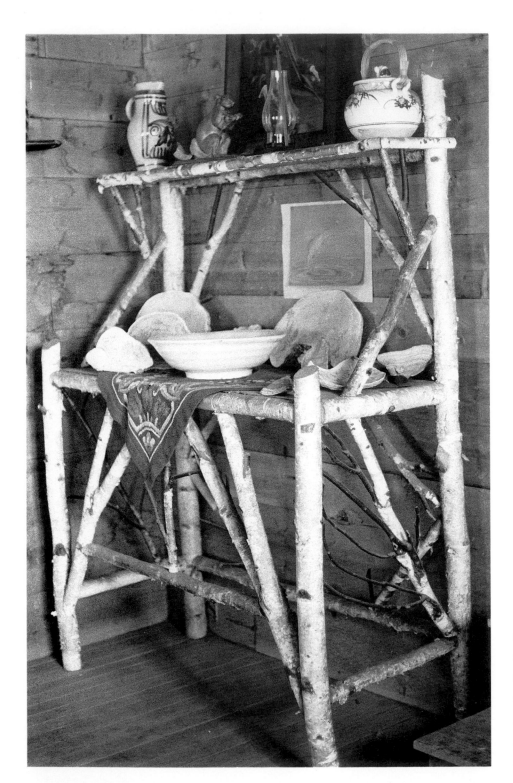

*53
Sideboard.
Chan Westcott (?),
Cranberry Lake.
Early 20th century.
Birch branch and
stick*

"The general principle at the Shanty was that if you wanted something you made it," recalled Elizabeth Putnam McIver of her years as a girl at her family's Putnam Camp in Keene Valley.[1] Resourcefulness was essential in the wilds. The simplest rustic furniture was made of sticks, resulting in the kind of seat or table anyone would contrive if given an ax or saw and sent into the woods. Since the 1820s visitors to the Adirondacks used such furniture, some of it fashioned by guides, to lend a modicum of comfort and civility to a camping trip. A typical excursion in the Adirondack wilds is commemorated by an 1886 photograph that shows two sportsmen in front of a lean-to, seated on log-and-slab benches at a table made of birch poles, eating a meal prepared by their guides (figure 39).

Stick furniture consisted of saplings or branches, commonly one to two inches in diameter and one to two feet long, that were nailed, wedged, or tied together to form tables and seats. For such furniture, function was more important than form. The maker of two chairs from Conifer, New York, quickly reached the limits of his material and imagination (figure 86). A man on fire watch atop the Blue Mountain tower was interested in utility, not elegance, when he assembled a chair from cherry sticks held together by nails and wire (figure 87). Stick furniture of this variety, with its "so-what" air, might be called "ramshackle rustic."

Ramshackle rustic describes furniture disparate in every way save for its indifference to appearances and the good opinion of the world. One is reminded of the "faintly disreputable air" which E. B. White discerned in summer cottages abandoned in the autumn, or the Latin motto on the crest of Lake Wobegon, Garrison Keillor's fictional Minnesota town: *Sumus quod sumus* (We are what we are). Some ramshackle furniture was stick, some used boards, some adopted a mix of wood and anything else that happened to be near at hand, as a sling chair of canvas and driftwood from Camp Sabael (plate 12). In the rocker and table made by Noah John Rondeau for his shanty home in Cold River country north of Long Lake (figure 89) is found the best embodiment of ramshackle as a principled statement about the life unvarnished.

But good-looking stick furniture that did not appear on the verge of collapse could be obtained. Hickory furniture from Indiana (see pages 240–251) is one example. Of Adirondack origin were chairs and tables made by Ernest Stowe, Lee Fountain, and Elmer Patterson (figures 62, 63, 67, 80, and plates 17–19), who favored yellow birch to the near exclusion of other wood. The bark of yellow birch "consists of thin,

Stick

papery layers that are reddish, according to the light, and as lustrous as satin," making it an aristocrat of rustic wood.[2] In addition to its iridescence and silky texture, characteristic of wood from saplings or immature trees, yellow birch has other virtues as well: strength and the adhesiveness of its bark to the branch.

White birch was also used for rustic furniture, though the wood is much less strong than yellow birch and has a tendency to get soft or "punky." A lodge on Cranberry Lake built about 1895 contains more white-birch rusticity than any other Adirondack camp the author has visited, including a sideboard in the dining room *(figure 53)*. Lake Placid Manor also has a set of locally made, modern white-birch furniture in one of its public rooms.

54
Bed and bureau.
Made by Ole Lynn
Snyder for his camp
on Lake Honnedaga.
1890–1914. Yellow
birch

55
*Side chair and
mirror with mosaic
twig frame. Both
made by Ole Lynn
Snyder for his camp
on Lake Honnedaga.
c. 1890–1914. The
chair of yellow birch
and the frame were
probably lost in the
fire that destroyed the
camp in 1980*

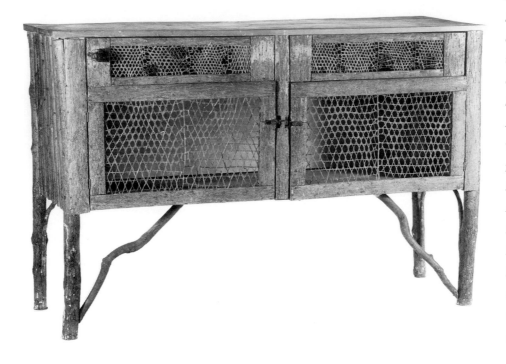

56

Sideboard. From a camp purchased by the Mitchell family c. 1900 on Upper Saint-Regis Lake. Ash, with rawhide woven in a snowshoe pattern, 40½ x 60⅝ x 22⅝". The Adirondack Museum. Gift of Mrs. Alfred H. Howell. Four fungi originally adorned the sideboard, but only one remains

ADIRONDACK
TREE
FURNITURE
86

57

Pair of armchairs. Upper Saint-Regis Lake. c. 1900. Ash and slippery elm, height 34⅝". The Adirondack Museum. Gift of Mrs. Alfred H. Howell. Horizontal leather thongs secure the twigs that comprise the backrest and sides. The maker may have exhausted his supply of rawhide (or patience) and resorted to twigs as an expedient alternative

58, 59

Reclining chair with adjustable footrest. c. 1900. Ash and slippery elm, length 50½". The Adirondack Museum. Gift of Mrs. Alfred H. Howell. The chair folds compactly for winter storage. The cradlelike arrangement at the end of the right arm holds a glass or tumbler

74

Lamp. Joseph Bryere, Raquette Lake. 1905. Birch, height 14¾".
The Adirondack Museum. Gift of Clara O. Bryere. This was a kerosene lamp that was converted to electricity

75

Hanging shelf. Bill Jones, Childwold Park Hotel, Childwold, New York. c. 1900. Yellow birch, height 32"

Plate 9

*A bench at the
boathouse, Camp
Topridge, c. 1920s*

Plate 10
Rocking chair.
Upper Saint-Regis
Lake. c. 1900. Ash
and slippery elm,
height 48½″. The
Adirondack
Museum. See figure
57 for companion
chairs

Plate 11
Child's rocking
chair. Northern New
York. Hickory with
splint seat and
leather wrapping
around the back and
arms, height 27"

Plate 12
Sling chair. Harry
E. Colwell, for Camp
Sabael, Indian Lake.
1908. Driftwood and
canvas, height 48".
The Adirondack
Museum. Gift of the
Colwell Family

*Plates 15
and 16
Armchair and
rocking chair.
Adirondacks.
Twentieth century*

Plate 17

Table. Ernest Stowe, Upper Saranac Lake. 1900–11. Birch bark and yellow birch, height 31"; top 43⅞" across. The Adirondack Museum. Warren M. Kay Collection. Written in pencil on the underside of the tabletop: "Price $15.00"

Plate 18

Table. Ernest Stowe, Upper Saranac Lake. 1900–11. Yellow birch with unfinished pine panel, height 30¾". The Adirondack Museum. Warren M. Kay Collection. A decorative cloth may have been intended to cover the plain pine panel

Plate 19

Chairs. Ernest
Stowe, Upper
Saranac Lake. 1900–
11. Yellow birch,
height about 38″.
The Adirondack
Museum. Warren M.
Kay Collection.
The double molding
around the edge of
each seat conceals the
ends of split rounds
and the wood slab to
which they are nailed

Plate 20

Armchair and stool.

Barry Gregson,

Schroon Lake, New

York. c. 1985

76–78

Bench and two
tables. Blue
Mountain Lake, New
York. After c. 1910.
Red maple: bench,
height 34⅜"; top
table, height 29⅞";
bottom table, height
27⁷⁄₁₆", top 28¼ x
32⅛". The
Adirondack Museum.
The furniture
was found in a
cottage on land
adjoining the Blue
Mountain House,
now site of the
Adirondack Museum

79

Porch, Camp
Ziegler, Loon Lake.
Photograph by
Chester D. Moses,
1908. The furniture
in the foreground
appears to be made of
wood from a shrub.
The camp burned
about 1970

80

Swing seat.
Covewood Lodge, Big
Moose Lake. c. 1925.
Yellow birch. Lee
Fountain made
swings like this

81

Bench. Camp of
Robert J. Collier,
Bluff Point, Raquette
Lake. 1913. Spruce,
overall width 18′11″.
The date "1913"
appears in log
segments just below
the arch at the top—
perhaps marking the
year that Robert J.
Collier, then-owner
of this camp and of
Collier's magazine,
built the recreation
building where the
bench is located

82–84
Chair. Lower Hudson
River Valley (?).
1850–90. Seaside
alder, painted black,
height 38¼".
The Adirondack
Museum. Gift of the
Onondaga Historical
Association.
Four similar pieces,
purchased in
Hudson, New York,
can be found at a
camp on Long Lake.
This chair came from
the summer home of
Lieutenant Governor
Thomas G. Alvord on
Governor's Island in
the St. Lawrence
River, near Clayton,
New York. Similar
workmanship
appears in an
illustration of a
mosaic and root
"Rustic Sofa" found
in a booklet
published in New
York in 1883

85
Postcard postmarked Baden-Baden, dated 1908 and addressed to Blue Mountain Lake. The bench is a prop in the studio of a German photographer. The message, from Mr. and Mrs. Ernest Ehrmann to friends in the Adirondacks, begins, "No fishing, no hunting, no boating here. . . ."

86

Chairs and table.
Conifer, New York,
region. Yellow birch,
height of table 28⅞".
The Adirondack
Museum. Gift of
Mr. and Mrs. G. Otis
Rockefeller.
From a set of four
chairs and a table

87

Side chair. Blue
Mountain Lake.
After 1960. Cherry
(reinforced by wire),
height 41¾".
The Adirondack
Museum. Gift of New
York State
Department of
Conservation

88, 89

Rocking chair and table. Noah John Rondeau, Cold River country. c. 1940. Scrap wood, height: chair, 38"; table, 31". The Adirondack Museum. The photograph shows Rondeau outside one of his two huts c. 1946. The rocker can be seen in the background

ADIRONDACK
TREE
FURNITURE
112

90

Side chairs. Abe Fuller. 1910–25. Yellow birch, height 35". Lake Placid– North Elba Historical Society, Lake Placid

91

"Aunt and Uncle" rocking chair. Abe Fuller. 1910–25. Willow (?), height 41½". Lake Placid– North Elba Historical Society. Gift of Deo B. Colburn. Fuller used this rocker at his shanty

effects, achieved at Camp Pine Knot, combined unbarked cedar with birch bark *(figures 103, 104, and plate 5)*. Unusual tables with cagelike cedar bases resemble tables illustrated in Victorian periodicals, but, as with mosaic twig work, the Adirondack examples were always more elaborate or cleverly contrived *(figures 106–113)*. A label beneath the seat of a cedar bench in Blue Mountain Lake states that it is to be shipped to the Holland House, a hotel that once operated in the hamlet. This may signify that the bench and its two companion pieces *(figures 114–116)*, like coal to Newcastle, may have been among those rustic products we may presume to have entered the Adirondacks by rail and road. "We are prepared to send skilled workmen to the Adirondacks and elsewhere," promised a 1902 catalogue by Dunne & Company, landscape architects and rustic builders with a salesroom in New York City. It is not surprising that rustic furniture came from outside the Adirondacks, since rustic workers in the region could not produce furniture in anything like the quantity needed to meet the demand.

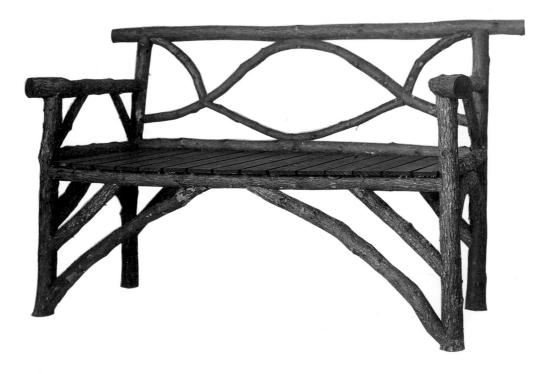

93

Bench. Will Young.

c. 1915–17. Cedar

94

Cedar bench, found on the porch of an
abandoned hotel in Aiden Lair, on the
highway between Minerva and Newcomb,
New York, 1974. Note the gentle
curves of the arms and cresting rail

98

Hutch. Blue Mountain Lake (?).
1882–1914. Cedar and applied birch
bark, 78 x 120 x 27". The Adirondack
Museum. Gift of Mr. Richard Van Yperen.
This sideboard, the largest free-standing
piece of rustic furniture known to the writer,
was made when Hiram Duryea still owned
his rustic camp on Blue Mountain Lake.
A subsequent owner recalled that the
sideboard was at the camp when the
property was turned into a hotel
in 1920–21

99

*Armchair. Made for
Camp Pine Knot,
Raquette Lake, 1880–
95. Cedar, height
43¾". A similar
chair photographed
on the porch of a
cottage at Brandreth
Lake (figure 1) is
surely by the same
maker. See plate 5*

100

*Desk. Walter
Turner (?), Camp
Minnewawa, Blue
Mountain Lake.
c. 1915 20. Cedar
and applied cedar
bark, height 30".
Turner worked at
Minnewawa as a
carpenter about 1918*

103

*Bed. Made for Camp
Pine Knot, Raquette
Lake. 1885–90.
Cedar and applied
birch bark, length
87". The Adirondack
Museum. Gift of
Raquette Lake Girls
and Boys Camp. A
companion of this
bed appears in
plate 5*

104

*Bed. Made for Camp
Pine Knot, Raquette
Lake, 1880–1900.
Cedar and applied
birch and cedar bark,
height of headboard
66⅛". The
Adirondack
Museum. Gift of
SUNY Cortland
Outdoor Education
Center*

*High-post bed. Camp
As-You-Like-It,
Brandreth Park.
1880–1900. Cedar,
length 84"*

110

Table. Made for Camp Pine Knot, Raquette Lake. 1876–95. Top of plain boards edged with cedar; pedestal of varnished cedar (the top was once covered with felt), height 28″

111

Table. Made for Camp Pine Knot, Raquette Lake. 1876–95. Top of plain boards with sides of applied birch bark framed by cedar; cedar pedestal, height 27″; width of top 48″. Underneath the tabletop is an inscription resembling the initials "FN"

112

Table. Made for Camp Pine Knot, Raquette Lake. 1876–95. Top of mosaic twig work with cedar base, height 28½". See figure 198 for view of top

113

Table. Made for Camp Pine Knot, Raquette Lake. 1876–90. Top of mosaic twig work with cedar base, height 27". The table was used in a combination bedroom and sitting room at Pine Knot

114–116
Bench and two
armchairs. Cedar. A
shipping label under
the seat of the bench
indicates that it was
shipped to the
Holland House in
Blue Mountain Lake

*by way of North
Creek, but no place
of origin is given.
The trio may come
from a manufacturer
of rustic furniture in
New York or New
England*

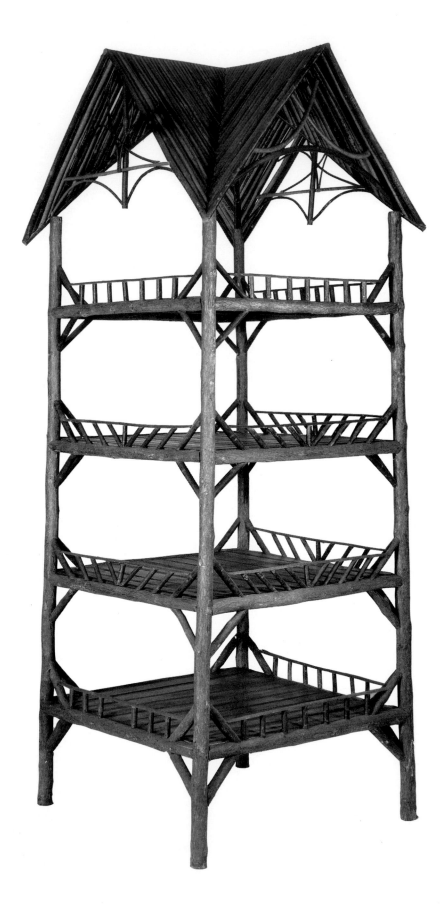

117

Covered stand. Made for Camp Pine Knot, Raquette Lake. 1876– 95. Cedar, striped maple, and other woods, 79½ x 27 x 27¾"

118–120

Four stands. Frank Alger, Eagle Nest, Blue Mountain Lake. c. 1935–40. Cedar, heights 42 to 72". The Adirondack Museum. Gift of Captain and Mrs. Boris Sergievsky

121
Rustic planter. New
York State (?).
c. 1850–1900. Cedar
with applied roots,
height 39". Margaret
Woodbury Strong
Museum, Rochester.
Similar planters
were sold by the
Rustique Work
Manufacturing
Company, Niagara
Falls, in the 1870s
and eighties

122
Making cedar
planters at Blue
Mountain House,
Blue Mountain Lake,
c. 1890

Woodbox. Made for
Camp Pine Knot,
Raquette Lake. 1876–
95. Cedar with
applied birch-bark
panels, height 20¾".
Destroyed by fire,
1983

124

Woodbox. Made for
Camp Pine Knot,
Raquette Lake. 1876–
95. Cedar with
applied birch-bark
panels, height 30"

125

Mrs. Woodruff's Room,

Kamp Kill Kare, Lake Kora, c. 1900.

This room and its contents were

probably destroyed in the fire of 1915.

Note the burl-topped table

ature yellow birch supplied most of the material for the root
bases and burl tops that identify a visibly distinctive group of
rustic furniture. The tree's predilection for sending roots
around rocks and rotting stumps, in search of a foothold in the
surrounding soil, created a natural form for the pedestals or bases of
tables and stands *(figures 127, 128, 130–34, 137, 138)*. One can imagine
guides and loggers taking mental note of trees having these elongated
"roots"—really the base of the tree extending as far as the soil line—
and returning to the locations later to cut and sell them to such rustic
workers as Fountain or Patterson. "I am writing to you on a table made
from the lower section and part of the root of a tree," says Lady Helen
Pole, a character in a 1901 book of fictional letters during a visit to an
Adirondack camp.[5]

126

*A burl on the trunk
of a yellow birch at
Camp Pine Knot*

Root
and Burl

Yellow birch and maples are susceptible to burls: unsightly but harm-
less growths caused by a reaction of the tree to infection or irritation,
as from insects *(figure 126)*. The burl, once removed from the tree,
would make a handsome tabletop. The cut side was sanded and stained,
and then varnished repeatedly to bring out the tight graining or figures
characteristic of burls. Two of the biggest burl tables were at Kamp
Kill Kare *(figures 125 and 128)*. To the skilled rustic worker, a burl is
what the oyster's pearl is to the jeweler.

127

*Table. Lewis H.
Porter (?), vicinity of
Inlet, New York.
c. 1910. Burl top and
root base of yellow
birch, height 27". The
table was in an old
camp on Seventh
Lake, where Porter
found employment*

128

*Table. Kamp Kill
Kare, Lake Kora.
1897–1925. Burl top
and root base of
yellow birch*

129

*"Living Room Cabin," Kamp
Kill Kare. Lake Kora, c. 1916–20.
In addition to the burl-top
table with root base in the
center of the room, note the
peeled-pole desk (figure 147) and
matching dressing table in the
corners, and the stuffed owl
perched on the balustrade above
the window. See figure 228 for
another view of this room*

130

*Table. Lee Fountain, Wells, New York.
c. 1915–30. Root base of yellow birch and
octagonal top with inlays of three or
four different woods, varnished;
height 28¼″, width of top 52″.*
History of Hamilton County *mentions
Fountain's "parquet-topped tables with
gnarled wooden legs [which] are still to be
seen in the older summer homes. . . ."*

131, 132

Table. Lee Fountain, Wells, New York. c. 1915–30. Top of varnished pine or spruce; root base of yellow birch, height 27¼", width of top 36". The Adirondack Museum.

Root bases were cut so they would stand flat on the floor by placing the stump in a sap pan of water and then cutting the roots precisely at the waterline. This table is not wobbly in the slightest

133

*Table. Joseph
Bryere, Raquette
Lake. 1905. Plain
board top and sides
of applied birch bark
framed by cedar; root
base of yellow birch;
height 31⅝"; top
31½ x 35¾".
The Adirondack
Museum. Gift of
Clara O. Bryere*

134

*Table. Joseph
Bryere, Raquette
Lake. 1895. Plain
board top with
applied birch bark
and lengths of cedar;
root base of yellow
birch; height 31¼";
top 18⅜ x 25⅛".
The Adirondack
Museum. Gift of
Clara O. Bryere*

135
Living room, D. W.
Wardwell camp,
Honnedaga Lake,
Adirondack League
Club, c. 1911. The
cottage and its rustic
work were probably
the work of a
photographer from
Utica named
Gardner. The property
was bought by the
Wardwells in 1914

136

Table. Mosaic twig work top;

root base of spruce (?).

The table was photographed on

the porch of the main lodge at Camp

Cedarlands, Long Lake, New York,

which has since burned down

137

*Table. George
Wilson (?), for
Sagamore Lodge,
Sagamore Lake.
1897–1925. Top of
mosaic twig work in
striped maple, witch
hazel, and birch,
with root base of
yellow birch, height
30¼".
The Adirondack
Museum. Gift of
Syracuse University.
See figure 200 for
view of top*

138

*Table. Blue
Mountain Lake (?).
1890–1920. Top of
mosaic twig work
with root base of
yellow birch. See
figure 204 for view
of top*

139

Bedroom, Kamp Kill Kare, Lake Kora, c. 1916–20.

After the lodge burned in 1915, Captain Charles Hiscoe, an

Englishman who had helped the Woodruffs decorate it earlier,

was invited by the second owners, the Francis P. Garvans, to

supervise the interior installations that replaced those

destroyed in the fire. For the chair on the right, see figure 142

When William West Durant started to build Camp Uncas in 1893, he may already have concluded that the bark-covered twig furniture at his own Camp Pine Knot, on nearby Raquette Lake, was impractical and too idiosyncratic for a speculative undertaking intended to appeal to prospective buyers. Camp Uncas was the first to use "production" rustic furniture, assembled from peeled poles of a generally consistent dimension that enabled multiple pieces to be made in a standard design. Beds of peeled-pole construction had previously appeared at camps on Raquette Lake *(figure 152 and plate 24)*, but these were individual efforts, unlike the furniture at Camp Uncas and later at Sagamore Lodge.

The peeled-pole furniture at Durant's later camps *(figure 151 and plate 1)* was treated with a stain whose formula was known only to him and his supplier, Cottier & Company, in New York City. In 1899, Durant wrote the superintendent at Sagamore Lodge to ask that an extra bedstead be made: "Frank Little [Durant's chief painter] can slip over some evening [from Pine Knot] and stain it, and then [stain it] again and wax it."[6] The furniture, in warm shades of reddish brown, blended nicely with paneled walls and giant peeled-log rafters. To this day, an odor of beeswax faintly emanates from the woodwork at Camp Uncas. Splashes of color were provided by red window curtains and red woolen blankets, maroon slipcovers, and several kinds of rug—from Navaho and Oriental to fur—on the floor.

Production furniture was an inevitable response to the problem of developing and then selling a camp to a buyer who insisted the property be ready for occupancy—beds in place, china and glassware in cabinets, running water, and the like. In contrast to Camp Pine Knot, which had evolved slowly, Camp Uncas required a concerted effort by Durant and his designers and workmen over a span of two or three years *(plate 1)*. He needed furniture that would be appropriate to Camp Uncas's rustic setting (by this time Pine Knot's rustic ambience had brought him minor fame), yet could be produced by workmen who might not be skilled in rustic work. Quantities of furniture, enough for fifteen rooms in four or five buildings, were needed. The result was a satisfactory compromise between factory-produced furniture available from stores and mail-order catalogues and the one-of-a-kind pieces that a handful of men had been turning out on Raquette Lake as their time and temperament allowed. Peeled-pole furniture had another advantage: it retained the rustic look that the builders and buyers of the Adirondack camps so dearly wanted, yet it was easy to maintain, a claim that could never be made for the dust-catching bark and twig variety.

Peeled Pole and Branch

140

Wall rack. Made by Ole Lynn Snyder for his camp at the Adirondack League Club, Lake Honnedaga. 1890–1914. Built on the wall, with peeled branches. The cottage and its furnishings were destroyed by fire in 1980

Durant used peeled-pole furniture at Sagamore Lodge, and a version of it was adopted by Timothy Woodruff when he furnished Kamp Kill Kare, several miles to the south, in 1897–1900 *(figure 125)*. Similar furniture soon began to appear in the Saranac Lakes region, at camps that Coulter and Westhoff designed for patrons like the copper tycoon Adolph Lewisohn. Coulter visited Sagamore Lodge in 1901 to prepare a plan for a recreation building there for the camp's new owner, Alfred G. Vanderbilt. Two or three years later, Coulter's firm installed beds in Lewisohn's camp that were similar to the peeled-pole models he had almost certainly seen at Sagamore Lodge.

Kamp Kill Kare had the widest selection of peeled-pole work in the Adirondacks. This camp, the grandest of the great-camp enclaves, contains elements dating back to 1897–1901, when fashionable rustic buildings were erected for the Woodruffs on land purchased from Durant. Kill Kare's rustic furnishings made it a showplace. Mr. and Mrs. Francis P. Garvan, who had bought the camp in 1914, rebuilt and greatly enlarged it after it burned down in 1915. The new rustic work attempted to recapture the rustic decor of the original camp.

141

Bench. In a camp at the Adirondack League Club, Lake Honnedaga. The cottage, log slab below with shingles above, was built c. 1895 for Robb De Peyster Tytus, possibly from a design by Stanford White, who also was a club member. The interior shows evidence of later alterations

142, 143

Sidechairs. Made for Kamp Kill Kare, Lake Kora. c. 1915–20. A softwood, probably pine or spruce, peeled and stained. Two of a set of three side chairs. They were used in a bedroom (figure 139)

ADIRONDACK
TREE
FURNITURE
150

The Garvans added furniture of peeled branches and limbs to the peeled-pole work of the Woodruff era. Most spectacular was a bed whose headboard was made of an entire tree, minus its bark, with a stuffed owl perched in its upper reaches *(figure 228)*. Mrs. Garvan's dressing table and desk, as well as chairs and benches, made good use of the many crooks in branches that had been peeled, smoothed, and lightly stained *(figures 129, 139, 142–47)*. Preparation of the furniture required considerable effort—of matching as nearly as possible one component with another, the cresting rails of two chairs, for example, or the arm rests of the same chair. But it was time well spent since the furniture was no more difficult to dust than the fine American and British antiques at the other Garvan residences.

Peeled-pole furniture was also installed in most of the rooms of a spacious log lodge built for Mr. and Mrs. Walter Hochschild in Blue Mountain Lake, New York. Completed in 1937, this was perhaps the last camp conceived and executed on a grand scale. The architect of the lodge was William Distin, but some of the furniture, of peeled spruce logs, whole and split, was fabricated from designs drawn by Kendall Rogers of Willsboro, New York *(figures 154 and plates 22, 23, 26, and 27)*. The furniture and interior woodwork of the lodge were of the same material and similarly treated. Honey-colored and pale-gray transparent stains, applied throughout, brought air and light to rooms that otherwise, with their heavy stone fireplaces and large scale, might have seemed oppressive.

144, 145
Recreation room,
Kamp Kill Kare,
Lake Kora, c. 1916–
20. The scale of this
cathedral-ceilinged
room called for a
fireplace and rustic
furniture of
comparable
proportion and
character. The chair
between the corner
windows (left) is
nearly six-feet tall.

146
Armchair. Made for
Kamp Kill Kare,
Lake Kora. 1915–20.
Possibly Eastern
spruce or Eastern
pine, peeled and
stained, 70½ x 44 x
24″

147
*Desk. Made for
Kamp Kill Kare,
Lake Kora. c. 1915–
20. Peeled softwood,
stained. Companion
piece to the dressing
table illustrated in
figure 129*

148
*Cabinet. Made for
Camp Uncas,
Mohegan Lake. 1893–
95. Peeled-pole
construction. This
piece was partly
based on the
watercolor illustrated
in figure 149*

149
*Watercolor design for
a cabinet dated June
1893, with the name
of William West
Durant written over
the name of the
young architect
Grosvenor Atterbury.
The Adirondack
Museum. Gift of
Mrs. Bromley Seeley*

150

Sleeping tent, Camp Wild Air, Upper Saint-Regis Lake, 1882. Tents on platforms were almost as comfortable as the cottages usually found nearby. Their novelty faded and eventually they were supplanted by permanent cabins, a few of which were painted with stripes to imitate their canvas predecessors. Note the peeled-pole bed with applied bark side panels

151

Bedroom, Camp

Uncas, Mohegan

Lake, 1895

152

Bed. Camp Oteewiti,
Raquette Lake, 1884–
1905, or Camp
Kwenogamac, Long
Lake, 1905–20.
Eastern white pine,
peeled-pole
construction,
73¼ x 80⅝".
The Adirondack
Museum. Gift of Dr.
John C. A. Gerster

153

*Dining-room chair.
Designed by Kendall
Rogers of Willsboro
and constructed in
Plattsburgh for
Eagle Nest, Blue
Mountain Lake.
1937–38. Unstained
spruce with buffalo
hide, height 37". One
of a set of eighteen
chairs*

154

*Table. See plate 23
for description*

155
Bed. Made for Kamp
Kill Kare, Lake
Kora. c. 1916–20.
Peeled branch,
unidentified wood

Plate 21
Armchair. England.
1760–1815. Yew,
height 34". The chair
is related to Windsor
furniture and
consists, with the
exception of the seat,
of knobby yew
branches that have
been peeled, stained,
and varnished.
An early example
of peeled-branch
furniture
construction

Plate 22

Dining room, Eagle

Nest, Blue Mountain

Lake, 1937–38.

William G. Distin

designed the lodge and

Kendall Rogers the

rustic furniture in this

late example of great-

camp construction in the

Adirondacks. One of

the chairs appears in

figure 153

Plate 23
Table. Designed by
Kendall Rogers
of Willsboro,
New York, and
constructed in
Plattsburgh for
Eagle Nest, Blue
Mountain Lake.
1937–38. Plain top,
spruce legs and
stretchers, height 30″;
top, extended, 35¼ x
16″. For a view
of the table open,
see figure 154

Plate 24
Bedroom, Echo Camp,
Raquette Lake, c. 1883.
The peeled-pole bed,
1883–1900, is 80" high.
The camp was originally the
summer residence of Governor
and Mrs. Phineas C.
Lounsbury of Connecticut

Plate 25
Built-in seating
of peeled-pole
construction, Manor
House, Camp Uncas,
c. 1893–95

Plate 26
Staircase at Eagle
Nest, built 1937–38,
with peeled-spruce
logs and trunks for
railings and risers

Plate 27
A window seat with
peeled-spruce work,
Eagle Nest, built
1937–38

156
Picture frame.
Birch bark and
sweet grass. Lake
Placid–North Elba
Historical Society

For centuries the Indians of North America had been fashioning shelters, boats, and containers from the ubiquitous tree. Wigwams and canoes were constructed of bark stripped from white birches and elms. In 1869 an English traveler described a birchbark shanty built on a promontory of Long Lake by Mitchell Sabattis, an Abanaki Indian who worked as a guide and was famed for his knowledge of the Adirondack wilds: "Three huge logs [formed the shanty's] three-sided foundations, defying rain and reptile. Four strong upright posts, with cross beams, compose its framework. Over these, broad sheets of white birch bark are thrown, clean, smooth and watertight. On its floor the twigs of fragrant hemlock boughs are strewn, making an elastic and pleasant bed." Sabattis's shelter was, the writer concluded, "certainly the chief of all birch-bark shanties [and] should stand in a book of art as a sample of purely native American architecture."[7] White hunters and settlers soon followed the Indians' example.

Spruce bark was a more typical covering for an improvised lean-to, open camp, or shanty *(figure 39)*. A more permanent version of this building, with walls, floor, and shingled roof of milled lumber, became a feature of the developed Adirondack camp by about 1880. The demand for bark for lean-tos was so great that campsites were marred by skeletal spruce trees that had died after sheets of bark had been peeled away from the base of their trunks.[8]

The use of bark for decorative purposes coincided with the appearance of great camps in the region. Camp Pine Knot, the earliest of the Adirondack camp enclaves, was the testing place for applying bark in novel but altogether plausible ways—inside buildings as well as outside *(plate 29)*. These treatments were widely adopted in the 1900s, notably for the large camps designed by the successive Coulter–Distin firms of 1897–1950. One of the last of the birch-bark-covered interiors is the octagonal dining room in a lodge on Eagle Lake designed by William Distin for Mr. and Mrs. Walter Hochschild in 1937–8 *(plate 22)*.

Bark is more durable than it looks, having a toughness not generally appreciated. When protected by overhanging eaves and deep porches, spruce- and cedar-bark coverings have endured for at least a half century, and repair material is no farther away than the nearby woods. Birch bark used indoors retains its color and body longer than wallpaper or paint. The bark ceiling of the Durant Cottage at Pine Knot is in fine condition today, though it was installed nearly ninety-five years ago *(plate 5)*. The disadvantage of bark is its combustibility, which probably kept it from being more widely used, though all log and wood-frame cottages were susceptible to fire in any case.

Applied Bark

The white birch supplied the bark most often applied to Adirondack furniture and interiors. An important example is a desk made for William West Durant around 1890, whose bark-veneered surfaces are ornamented with diamonds, triangles, stars, and hearts outlined by split twigs of shadbush or striped maple *(figures 163 and 164)*. The contrasting tones of the two sides of the bark—white and tan—serve to emphasize the pattern.

Joseph Bryere, who produced a quantity of birch-bark furniture (including, perhaps, this desk), achieved similar contrasts on a tall clock case, using a checkerboard pattern to embellish each side of the case *(figure 186)*. The design was fashioned by weaving tissue-thin strips of outer-facing bark with strips of inner-facing bark. The device is as obvious as it is effective, yet the author has not seen plaited bark elsewhere.

Another important group of birch-bark furniture was made by Ernest Stowe in the early 1900s for Isaac Simonin's Camp Ninomis on Second Stony Creek Pond near Upper Saranac Lake. Combining birch bark with yellow-birch segments, Stowe made case pieces whose form and decoration derive from eighteenth-century cabinetwork. The quar-

157

Spruce bark being replaced on a privy from Camp Kwenogamac, Long Lake, 1905–20

158

Lamp table. Made by Ole Lynn Snyder for his camp at the Adirondack League Club, Lake Honnedaga, 1890–1914. Yellow birch. The camp and other furnishings were destroyed in a fire. The walls are covered with yellow-birch bark; the Mottville side chair has distinctive black bands

ter columns, cornices, and recessed panels of his secretaries and sideboards *(figures 171, 172, and plate 33)* clearly reveal this influence, as do the star and sunburst motifs worked out in yellow birch. (As is typical of rustic furniture, the sides of the drawers are nailed together, not dovetailed.) Several pieces of Stowe furniture belong to an old camp in Hamilton County *(figures 167, 169, and 170)*, and a Lake Placid dealer recently found other examples. Stowe's hand was sure and he had a sensitive eye for proportion and contrast. His furniture has perhaps the most ambitious aspirations of any to transcend its rustic station. This seems to have been underscored in 1986 when a dining-room table and twelve chairs and a sideboard were knocked down at auction for a total of $69,000, the highest sum ever paid for rustic furniture.[9]

159

*Table. Blue
Mountain Lake.
1880–1910. Plain
board top; cedar legs
and braces and
applied cedar bark
on frame and legs, 31
x 62 x 28". The table
is in the main
residence of the
summer home
originally built for
General Hiram
Duryea in 1880–82.
The property became
a hotel, The Hedges,
in 1920–21*

Applied cedar bark was second to birch in its use by Adirondack craftsmen. A tall case made by Joseph Bryere in 1887 employs cedar bark around the clock face *(figure 224)*, and a bed from Camp Pine Knot has a cedar-bark panel on its footboard *(figure 104)*. A desk and a table in Blue Mountain Lake incorporate a considerable quantity of cedar bark *(figures 100 and 159)*. But on the whole, cedar bark was not applied to furniture. It was widely used, however, on the exteriors of buildings at camps Pine Knot and Uncas and Sagamore Lodge.

Few rustic workers used the bark of the yellow birch in their furniture. The most ambitious example known to the author is a hutch at Camp Pine Knot *(plate 31)*, which reveals the bark's deficiency, its tendency to split and curl as it dries. This did not trouble Ole Lynn Snyder, who covered the walls of the sitting room in his cottage on Honnedaga Lake with yellow-birch bark *(figure 158)*.

Bark was serviceable as an exterior siding, and it was pressed into duty as a covering for interior walls and even ceilings. Spruce bark was most commonly used outside, to judge from contemporary photographs, perhaps because it was plentiful and tough. When cut in large sheets in spring and early summer and then weighted down to soak in a stream, it emerges as pliable as a tanned cowhide. Spruce bark seems to have been used to wrap ceiling beams at a camp designed by William Coulter *(figure 49)*, but the use of spruce indoors was unusual, probably because the bark was dark in color and its scaly surface tended to shed when it wasn't harboring bugs and dust. A chest of drawers at Camp Wild Air is covered with spruce bark—the only example known to the author *(plate 30)*. Cedar bark was used abundantly at William West Durant's camps, but on outside walls only. The dining room of Camp As-You-Like-It, where the walls are sheathed with cedar bark from floor to ceiling, shows that this material can be successfully used inside *(plate 30)*. Cedar bark is easily worked, soft to the touch, and reddish brown in color; these assets are offset by its fibrous surface, which also sheds and collects dust.

Birch bark possessed all of the advantages of spruce and cedar with none of their handicaps. It looked clean, was relatively easy to dust, did not shed, and its whiteness brightened dark camp interiors. Like the other barks, white-birch bark was peeled from trees between March and July and applied fresh (it loses its suppleness as it dries, becoming more difficult to handle).

160

Chest of drawers. Attributed to Nelson Dunn. Pine case with cedar shingles and rustic handles, height 32". This is one of five shingled pieces that originally belonged to the owner's father at a cottage, since demolished, on Cascade Lake

161

*Bookcase. Made for
Camp Pine Knot,
Raquette Lake,
c. 1885–95. Cedar
with applied white-
and yellow-birch
bark, varnished,
height 75 ½".
Destroyed in the fire
at Pine Knot in 1983*

162

*Living room, Swiss
Cottage, Camp Pine
Knot, Raquette Lake.
1893. Note the rustic
cupboard (plate 31),
here used as a
bookcase*

163, 164

Kneehole desk. Made for William West Durant, Camp Pine Knot, Raquette Lake. 1885–95. Applied birch bark with split-twig trim of cedar, cherry, shadbush, and striped maple, 28 x 58 x 31". Note monogram "WD" in kneehole. False drawers on the left panel decorate a door that opens on a compartment

165

*Washstand. Joseph Bryere, Raquette Lake. 1895. Applied birch bark and split-twig trim, height 38".
The Adirondack Museum. Gift of Clara O. Bryere*

166

Dresser. Joseph Bryere, Raquette Lake. 1897. Applied birch bark and split-twig trim of shadbush, height 74¼".
The Adirondack Museum. Gift of Clara O. Bryere. Between the adjustable mirror and its backing is a fragment of the newspaper The New York Press *for February 24, 1897. As with nearly all other pieces by Bryere illustrated in these pages, this dresser was among the furnishings at the hotel, Brightside-On-Raquette, opened by him and his wife about 1891*

167

*Sideboard. Ernest
Stowe, Upper
Saranac Lake.
c. 1904. Applied
white-birch bark with
trim of yellow birch,
78¾ x 52¾ x 26¾".
The watercolor scene
bears the inscription:
"Decorated by/
Mother Nature/ +
M.C. [unreadable
surname]." Below is
the date "1904"*

168

Living room, Bull Cottage, an installation at the Adirondack Museum in a turn-of-the-century camp. All of the furniture is of Adirondack origin. See figures 62, 186, 205, and plates 33 and 42 for pieces included in this photograph

169, 170

Secretary. Ernest

Stowe, Upper

Saranac Lake.

c. 1904. Applied

white-birch bark with

yellow-birch trim,

70¼ x 45 x 24"

171, 172
Secretary. Ernest
Stowe (?), Camp
Ninomis, Upper
Saranac Lake. 1900–
11. White-birch bark
and applied yellow
birch, 72½ x 43 x
25¾". The
Adirondack
Museum. Warren W.
Kay Collection

173
Sideboard.
D. Savage (?).
Saranac Lake. 1910–
30 (?). Applied birch
bark and cedar twig
trim, height 72⁵⁄₁₆".
The Adirondack
Museum. Gift of
International Paper
Company.
The attribution is
based on its
association with the
desk (figure 175)
from the same camp
on Bog Lake. Below
the drawer on the
right is a door with
false drawer fronts
opening into a
compartment with a
single shelf

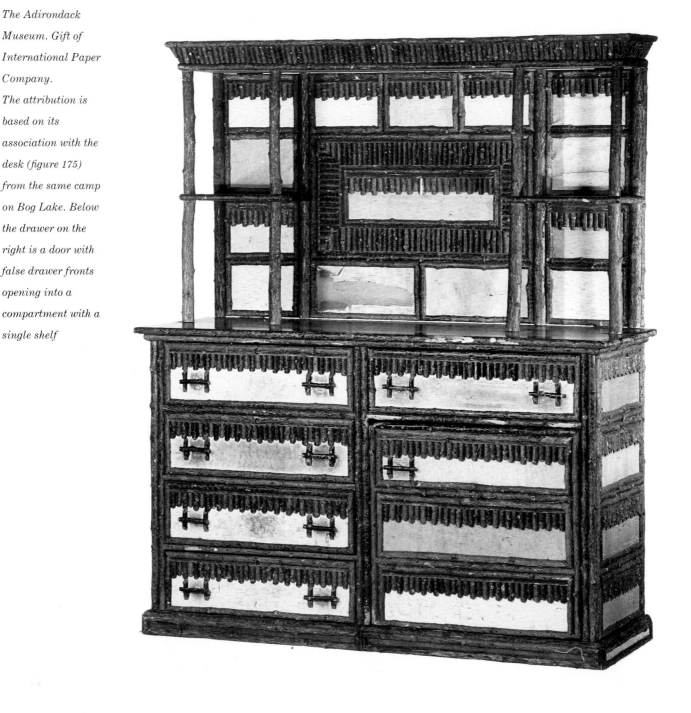

174, 175
Kneehole desk.
D. Savage, Saranac
Lake. 1910–30 (?).
Applied birch bark
and twig trim
of cedar,
height 29⅞″.
The Adirondack
Museum. Gift of
International Paper
Company. On the
underside of the top
drawer is the stamp:
"D. Savage /
Manufacturer of all
kinds / of / Rustic
Furniture, Saranac
Lake, N.Y.,"
enclosed within a
rustic gate

176

Sideboard.
D. Savage (?),
Saranac Lake. 1910–
30 (?). Applied
balsam (?) bark and
trim of Eastern
spruce, height 46¾".
The Adirondack
Museum. Gift of
International Paper
Company.
The attribution is
based on the
association of this
sideboard with the
desk bearing
Savage's stamp
(figure 175) from the
same camp on Bog
Lake. The only piece
the author has seen
with bark of this kind

Plate 28
*Now a sunporch at
The Hedges hotel,
Blue Mountain Lake,
this may originally
have been a summer
dining room for the
Duryea Camp, built
in the 1880s. Of
spruce, cedar, and
birch with applied
vines and twigs, it is
a rustic gem despite
its run-down
condition. See figure
236 and plate 37*

Plate 29
Bay window with
applied bark and
twig trim, Recreation
Building, Camp Pine
Knot, c. 1895

Plate 30
Chest of Drawers.
Camp Wild Air,
Upper Saint-Regis
Lake. Before 1900 (?).
Spruce bark was
applied to the chest,
which was originally
painted in an imitation
wood-grain pattern,
height 33"

Plate 31

A corner of the recreation building, Camp Pine Knot. The hutch, 1880–93, is veneered with yellow-birch bark and trimmed with cedar and other woods. Yellow-birch bark was barely used on rustic furniture, because it tended to shrink and split. The cypress chair dates from about 1948

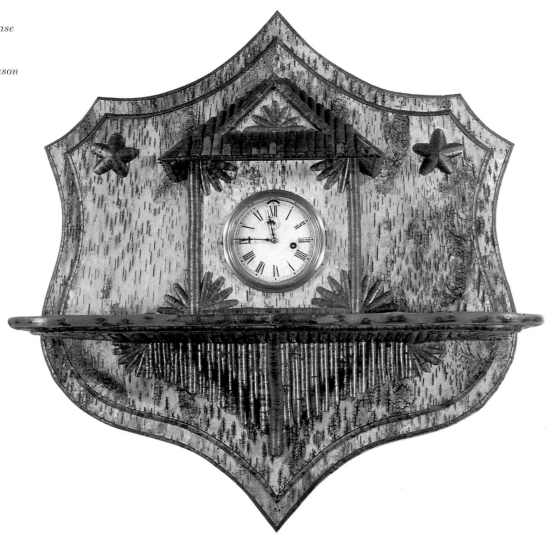

Plate 33
Sideboard. Ernest Stowe, for Camp Ninomis (?), Upper Saranac Lake. 1900–11. Applied white-birch bark with trim of yellow birch, 86¾ x 59½ x 28½". The Adirondack Museum. Warren W. Kay Collection

Plate 34

*Bookcase. Ernest Stowe, Upper
Saranac Lake. 1900–11. Applied white-
birch bark with trim of yellow birch,
76⅝ x 50⅛ x 14". The Adirondack
Museum. Warren W. Kay Collection.
Stowe's fondness for framing white-
birch bark with yellow-birch
trim is especially effective in this
well-proportioned bookcase.
The hooflike feet offer just the
right counterthrust to the cornice above*

Plate 35

*Desk. Ernest Stowe,
Upper Saranac Lake.
1900–11. Varnished
pine desktop and
shelf with applied
white-birch bark and
yellow-birch trim;
cedar legs and
stringers,
54½ x 43⅝ x 25".
The Adirondack
Museum. Warren W.
Kay Collection*

Plate 36

Dining room, Camp As-You-Like-It. Originally a one-room house built by a trapper about 1840, this small cottage was later moved and attached to the kitchen at Camp As-You-Like-It, where it became the dining room. The cedar bark was applied about 1900, when the Craftsman-style furniture was purchased

Hamper and box.
Blue Mountain
Lake (?). 1900–25.
Peeled-pole frames
and applied birch
bark, height of
hamper 35".
The Adirondack
Museum. Gift of
William Wessels

APPLIED

BARK

193

178

Jewelry box. Joseph
Bryere, Raquette
Lake. 1887. Twig
trim on applied birch
bark, 6⅛ x 9½".
The Adirondack
Museum. Gift of
Clara O. Bryere.
Bryere probably
made the similar box
seen on the table in a
photograph of the
living room at the
Stott camp (figure
237) where he and his
wife were employed
in 1887–90

179
Frame. c. 1877–95.
Applied birch bark
with striped-maple
trim, 17½ x 25½".
The Adirondack
Museum. Gift of
SUNY Cortland
Outdoor Education
Center. Levi Wells
Prentice, who
painted this view of
Raquette Lake,
worked in Syracuse,
Buffalo, and New
York City. He visited
the Adirondacks
often between 1873
and the early eighties

180
Frame. Joseph
Bryere, Raquette
Lake. Before 1900 (?).
Applied birch bark
with cedar trim. The
painting, of Raquette
Lake, may have been
painted by Bryere
after he retired and
began wintering
in Florida

181

*Frame. Made for
Camp Pine Knot,
Raquette Lake. 1885–
90. Applied birch
bark with cedar trim,
33½ x 27". This
mirrored frame hung
in the bedroom of
Mr. and Mrs.
William West
Durant and remains
at Pine Knot today*

182

*Frame. Applied
birch bark with trim
of cedar, striped
maple, and
branchlets, 9 x 19"*

ADIRONDACK
TREE
FURNITURE
196

*184
Frame. Lake Placid.
Applied birch bark
with sweet-grass
trim. The
Adirondack
Museum. Gift of
Grace and Eleanor
Nitzschke. The use of
sweet grass as a trim
suggests that the
frame was produced
by Indians for sale to
summer tourists*

185

Plaque with mirror,
shelf, and drawer.
Ernest Stowe, Upper
Saranac Lake. 1900–
11. Applied white
birch bark with
yellow-birch trim,
height 40"

186

*Clock case. Joseph
Bryere, Raquette
Lake. c. 1895.
Applied birch bark
and split twigs, one
being shadbush,
height 95".
The Adirondack
Museum. Gift of
Clara O. Bryere. The
word "Osceola,"
probably for the
camp of that name
built about 1895 for
John N. Golding,
was worked out in
twigs on the panel
above the upper door.
The three-part case
has shelving in the
middle compartment*

187

*Clock case.
Made for Horace
Inman, Raquette
Lake. c. 1894–1915.
Birch, applied birch
bark and twig trim,
height 34⅜". The
clock was
manufactured in
Connecticut by the
Seth Thomas
Company. The "69"
on the face may refer
to Inman's age*

188

Living room of the principal

cottage at Horace Inman's camp,

Raquette Lake, c. 1900–15.

The clock on the mantel

is illustrated in figure 187.

Horace Inman came to Raquette

Lake in 1894 and built the

most exotic camp complex

in the Adirondacks,

mixing rustic, American

Indian, and Japanese styles,

all evident in this photograph

The most refined expressions of Adirondack rustic craft are the sideboards, cabinets, and tables whose surfaces were decorated with what British writers variously termed "mosaic work," "pattern work," and "wood mosaic." The technique, more easily described than done, called for straight, regular twigs to be cut in half lengthwise and tacked to a design drawn in pencil on a wood-slab base. "The pieces are nailed to any flat surface of wood," explained an English magazine in 1834, "and very beautiful and elaborate patterns may be produced by arranging the pieces according to their sizes and the various colours of the bark."[10] The kaleidoscope of geometric patterns in mosaic work, one design never duplicating another but each composed of variations of the triangle, circle, and square, impresses the viewer and arouses the same admiration and curiosity as quilt work of the period. Indeed, the baskets worked out in twigs on the corner cupboard at the Adirondack Museum *(figure 205)* may have been borrowed from a quilt pattern called "Flower Basket." However, the elaborate designs of tabletops and case pieces were basically local compositions by individual makers. Opportunities for invention were endless: there are eight different arrangements of twigs on the sides of the octagon formed by the top of a table from Sagamore Lodge *(figures 137 and 200)*. Fertile variation also characterizes the pedestals which support the tops of many mosaic-top tables. No two of the cagelike supports have the same construction.

Surely patience and concentration were needed for this work. The variegated pattern of a corner cupboard made for Camp Cedars combines twigs from ten varieties of trees and shrubs *(figure 205)*. Other important examples of mosaic work are found on two giant sideboards, one at Bluff Point Camp *(figure 207)* and one at Trophy Lodge *(figure 206)*. A smaller sideboard, in the Bissell family house on Long Lake since the late nineteenth century and reliably attributed to Andrew Fisher incorporates representations of a log cabin and two open camps into its mosaic twig veneer *(figures 209 and 210)*.

The focal point for mosaic twig work was Raquette Lake, with outlying centers at Brandreth and Forked lakes to the north, Blue Mountain and Long lakes to the east, and Mohegan, Sagamore, and Kora lakes—each having a great camp on its shore—to the south. Mosaic furniture was also made elsewhere (Mildred Phelps Stokes recalled seeing "rustic work . . . made up of many small pieces of bark-covered wood" at her parents' camp on Upper Saint-Regis Lake in the 1890s[11]), but outside of this central Adirondack area little of equal quality and quantity has turned up.

Poplar Grove Church, Petersburg, Virginia, March 5, 1865. Albumen photograph by Timothy H. O'Sullivan, from Alexander Gardner's Photographic Sketchbook of the Civil War *(1866). It was proposed that the log-and-pole structure be moved to Central Park in New York City, but nothing came of the idea*

Mosaic Twig Work

190, 191

*Two views of Sunset
Cottage, formerly at
Camp Cedars, now
on Little Forked
Lake*

Mosaic work was also used occasionally for architectural ornamentation, to decorate overmantels and the outsides of cottages. The fireplace at Trophy Lodge still retains the mosaic panel that was constructed above the mantel between 1875 and 1885 *(plate 38)*. And the gable wall of one of the earliest buildings at Brandreth Park, now shingled, was once decorated with split poles or rods in a herringbone pattern. The small Sunset Cottage salvaged from Camp Cedars after the Great Blowdown hurricane of 1950, sheathed on all four sides by split rods, is the finest surviving example of mosaic twig *(figures 190 and 191)*. The

cottage was skidded across the ice to its present location near the Adirondack house of Mr. and Mrs. C. V. Whitney.

Rustic mosaic work, suitable in every respect to eighteenth-century tastes, may have been invented in England and was a special feature of the English garden (see pp. 29–30). How the mosaic technique found its way to the Adirondacks may never be known. The rustic officers' quarters and chapel erected at the field posts of Union troops at Petersburg and Beverly Ford, Virginia, are possible sources of influence (*figure 189*). "Had service in our new rustic chapel," wrote John L. Cunningham in his diary entry for February 28, 1864, at a Union encampment in eastern Virginia.[12] Cunningham's regiment, the 118th New York Volunteers Infantry, was mustered in Essex County, while Seth Pierce, who later made rustic furniture for the Durant family and others, was recruited for the 169th New York Volunteers in Warren County, which adjoined on the south. However, Joseph Bryere, who also produced mosaic furniture, did not serve in the Civil War, having been born in Quebec in 1859. The Durants and their friends who came to the Adirondacks in the 1870s may provide another source of influence, for early photographs of camps Pine Knot and Cedars show rustic furniture in use, including pedestal tables with mosaic tops (*figure 45*).

192

Living room, Trophy Lodge, Brandreth Park, c. 1880. Pictured are General Edwin A. McAlpin, who built Trophy Lodge c. 1872, and his wife, Annie. The mosaic twig overmantel was probably the work of whoever made the sideboard at Trophy Lodge (figure 206). For a contemporary view of the room, see plate 38

193
Table. Long Lake.
Top of mosaic twig
work with cedar base

194
Table. Made for
Camp Pine Knot,
Raquette Lake. 1876–
95. Top of mosaic
twig work and
applied birch bark,
cedar base, height 28"

195

Table. Joseph Asher,
Blue Mountain Lake.
1902. Mosaic twig
base and hexagonal
top overlaid with
birch bark and
trimmed with small
pine cones,
height 29¾".
The Adirondack
Museum. Inscribed
in pencil under the
top: "Joe Asher/April
the/5 1902." Asher
was employed by
William West
Durant as head
ship's carpenter in
1901. A photograph
of Camp Cedars
taken about 1885
(figure 45) shows a
table similar to this
one. The decoration
with pine cones is
unusual

196

Table. Charles
Vandenberg (?), Blue
Mountain Lake.
c. 1900. Top of
mosaic twig work
and applied spruce
bark, cedar legs and
supports, trim of
other woods,
height 30¼".
The Adirondack
Museum. Gift of Mr.
and Mrs. Paul
Maloney. See figure
199 for view of top

198

Mosaic twig

table top.

See figure 112

for a description

of the table

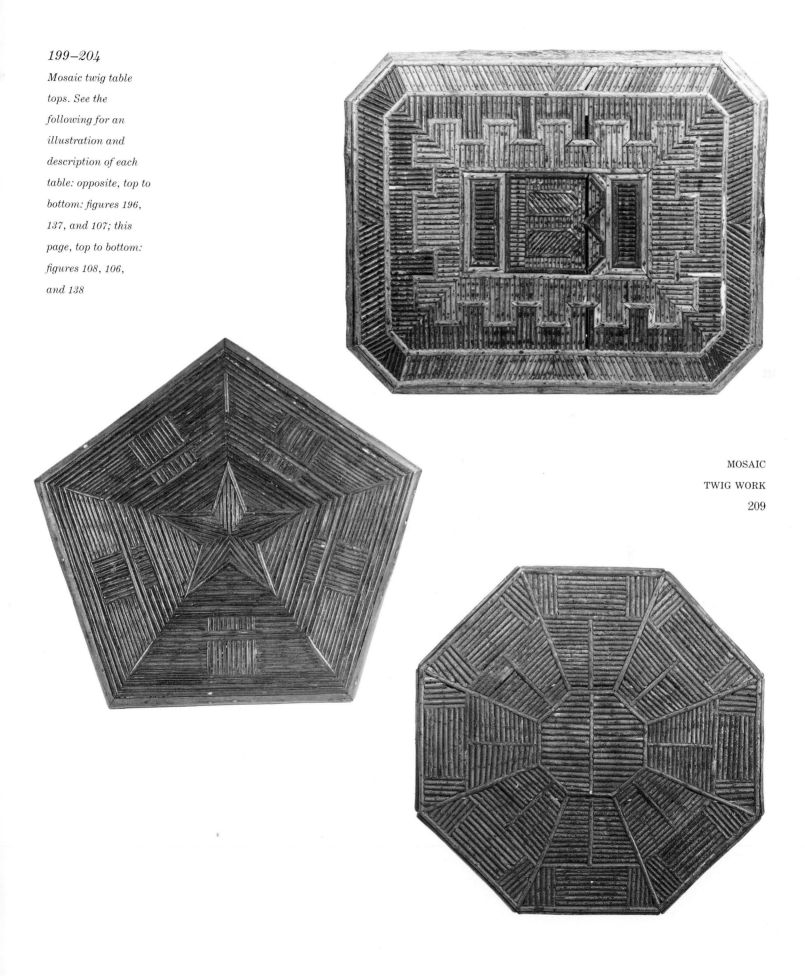

199–204

*Mosaic twig table
tops. See the
following for an
illustration and
description of each
table: opposite, top to
bottom: figures 196,
137, and 107; this
page, top to bottom:
figures 108, 106,
and 138*

205

Corner cupboard.
Seth Pierce, Camp
Cedars, Little Forked
Lake. c. 1880–90.
Mosaic twig work,
70⅝ x 44".
The Adirondack
Museum. Gift of
Frederick Clark
Durant, Jr.
Twigs from ten
varieties of trees and
shrubs were used on
this cupboard: three
maples (sugar,
swamp, and striped);
yellow and white
birch; and beech,
ash, wild cherry,
shadbush, and witch
hazel. The pattern is
derived from a
nineteenth-century
quilt design known
as Flower Basket

206

Sideboard. Seth Pierce, Trophy Lodge, Brandreth Park. c. 1880–90. Mosaic twig work, 81 x 75 x 27¾". The sideboard appears in a photograph of Brandreth family members taken on the porch of Trophy Lodge (figure 52)

207

Sideboard. Seth Pierce or Joseph Bryere, for the Bluff Point Camp of Frank H. Stott. Raquette Lake. c. 1885–90. Mosaic twig work, 82 x 74¼ x 30¼". The attribution to Pierce is based on its similarity to the sideboard in figure 206, but Bryere worked at Bluff Point in the 1880s

208

*Parlor, Endion, Long
Lake. c. 1900. Residents
generally preferred
conventional homes, with
plaster and wallpaper walls.
This contrasted with
summer residents, for
whom "getting away"
meant "primitive"
interiors. See
figure 209 for the
sideboard in the far room*

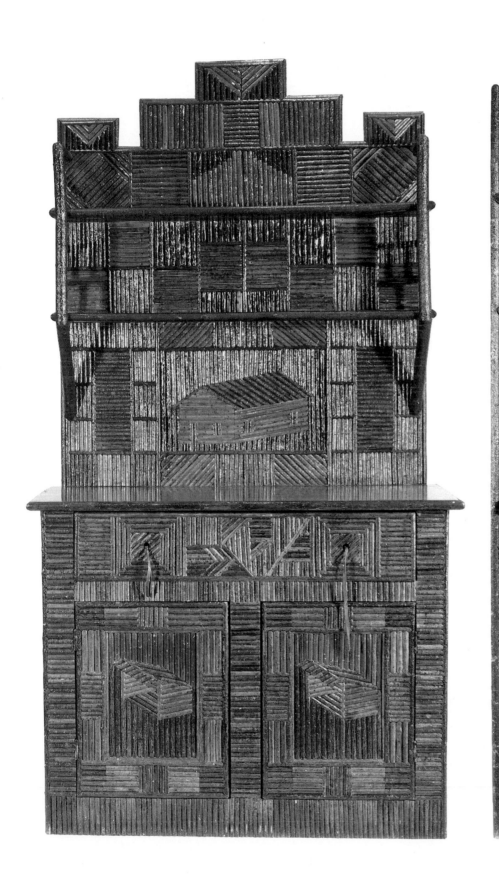

209, 210
Sideboard. Andrew Fisher, Endion, Long Lake. c. 1890–95. Mosaic twig work, 62 x 53 x 17½". Endion was a residence and hotel belonging to the Bissell family. The sideboard appears in a photograph taken there about 1900 (figure 208). A log cabin and two open camps are used as decorative motifs

211, 212

Settee. Camp Uncas,
Mohegan Lake. 1893
or after. Mosaic twig
work, striped maple
painted black, height
41½". The
Adirondack Museum

ADIRONDACK
TREE
FURNITURE
214

213

Settee. George Wilson (?), Sagamore Lodge, Sagamore Lake. 1897 or after. Mosaic twig work, Eastern cottonwood (?) painted black, height 39¾". The Adirondack Museum. Gift of Syracuse University. The reverse of the backrest is lined with a thin fabric held by long lengths of split twigs to the board base

214

Settee. Made for the Bluff Point camp built and occupied by the Stott family, Raquette Lake. 1878– c. 1905. Mosaic twig work. The twig work on the seat has been removed. The cusped molding of the backrest is a nice touch

215
Frame. Mosaic twig
work, height 7⅝".
The Adirondack
Museum. Gift of
Mrs. Alfred B.
Thacher.
From an early camp
on Blue Mountain
Lake

ADIRONDACK
TREE
FURNITURE
216

216
Frame. Saranac
Lake area. Mosaic
twig work, striped
maple, 15½ x 15½".
The Adirondack
Museum

217

Frame. Camp Pine Knot. c. 1876–95. Mosaic twig work with branchlets applied around the perimeter, 10 x 14". Destroyed by fire, 1983

218

Frame. Echo Camp, Raquette Lake. 1883–1900. Mosaic twig work

219

Humidor. Raquette Lake. 1885–95. Mosaic twig work and applied birch bark, 6¾ x 11½". The Adirondack Museum. Gift of Mrs. W. W. Durant. The humidor was probably made for William West Durant

ADIRONDACK
TREE
FURNITURE
218

220

Box. Schroon Lake (?). Twigs of striped maple

221, 222

Sewing box. Fourth Lake. Applied twigs for logs and bark for the roof, painted or varnished; fabric lining inside is Japanese, 14 x 10¾". The Adirondack Museum. Gift of H. Burhans

223

Clock case. Bill Jones (?). Childwold, New York. c. 1888–1910. Mosaic work of yellow-birch segments, height 13⅝". The Adirondack Museum. Gift in memory of Miss Nanette Ehrmann. The clock, an alarm clock with a large bell on top, sits on an interior shelf and may be removed

224
Clock case. Joseph
Bryere, Raquette
Lake. 1887. Mosaic
twig work and
applied birch and
cedar barks.
The case was
constructed from a
crate bearing the
stencil of a piano
manufacturer in
Boston

While Victorian women grew misty-eyed over wildlife depicted in paintings, prints, and the popular press in the last half of the century, their men embarked on eradicating whole populations of deer, bison, waterfowl, and other animal life from the face of the earth. This mindless slaughter, involving both commercial hunters who sold meat to city restaurants and sportsmen mimicking upper-class British customs, would eventually require a combination of game laws, the creation of state and national park preserves, the emergence of humane and ecologically focused scientists and politicians, and an informed citizenry, to curb it in the United States.

Indeed, the need for protection in the Adirondacks became apparent by the 1870s. The moose, once abundant, was no longer to be found; the beaver, a New York symbol since the seventeenth century, was disappearing; and fish, principally trout, were scarce in many streams and lakes where once they had been plentiful. Alvah Dunning had boasted that he and his father and two other hunters had killed a hundred moose in the winter of 1838: "I killed the last moose and trapped the last beaver that ever roamed the woods or dammed a stream in the lower Adirondack region." The guide, recalling these days at the age of seventy-nine, credulously marveled, "It's queer how sudden and mysterious the moose disappeared from the woods over south. The last year of the war [1865] the woods were full of them. It seemed as if I could shoot one at almost every turn."[13]

Evidence of the hunt is plain to see in commissioned photographs of interiors of baronial city homes constructed for Gilded Age families to display their status and wealth. Mounted heads of antelope, lions, water buffalo, and other big game greeted visitors in high-ceilinged stair halls and assembly rooms of town houses between Boston and Chicago. In the Adirondacks, a few larger camps sported trophies brought from outside the region. Among the more notable were Trophy Lodge, built by General Edwin A. McAlpin at Brandreth Park starting about 1875 *(plate 38);* the living room of William Seward Webb's sprawling shingle-style lodge, constructed at Nahasane in 1890–91; the rustic recreation building designed for Alfred G. Vanderbilt at Sagamore Lodge in 1901 and embellished by his widow, Margaret Emerson; and the cathedral-ceilinged living room of the lodge at Camp Topridge, the summer home built for Marjorie Post (then Mrs. E. F. Hutton) on Upper Saint-Regis Lake in 1923 *(plate 8).*

The champion among such Adirondack places, however, is the castle built at the edge of Lake Madeleine in 1910–13 for Edward H. Litchfield

225

Two raccoons in the branches of a tree, "Living Room Cabin," Kamp Kill Kare, Lake Kora, c. 1916–20

226

Stuffed bear cub under an eave outside a window, "Living Room Cabin," Kamp Kill Kare. The bear peers into the room shown in figures 129 and 228

of Brooklyn, New York. Constructed of stone, the lodge has a two-story hall containing mounted specimens of game bagged in Africa, Great Britain, and Asia—as well as the Adirondacks. Nearly one hundred and ninety animal trophies are said to be scattered through at least fifty rooms in the lodge, in the heart of Mr. Litchfield's carefully managed game and forest preserve.

Since the white-tailed deer was the prize game for resident and non-resident hunters alike, most camps, hotels, and homes in the Adirondacks displayed evidence of successful hunts in the nearby woods. Deer heads and antler racks lined walls and crowned chimney breasts (*figures 49, 125, 145, 237, 260, and 265*). Deer hooves were used as the feet of stools; when bent at the ankle with the hoof pointed upward, they served as racks for holding rifles and shotguns (*figure 231*). Large trout were mounted on wooden plaques, often with a copper plate label giving the date and location of capture. In 1908, Oliver Kemp recommended snowshoes, paddles, a game head, or mounted fish for the wall, and furs on the floor. These, he said, referring to suitable decorations for a wilderness vacation home, "give the last note of the woodsy flavor." [14]

Smaller creatures did not escape unscathed. At the summerhouse of Hiram Duryea on Blue Mountain Lake, stuffed birds, a raccoon head, and a chipmunk were incorporated into the rustic frieze above the windows and doors of a glassed-in dining building *(plate 38)*. A reading nook at Kamp Kill Kare, dating from 1915–20, has stuffed songbirds perched on the branches of a tree *(figure 227)*, while an owl with outstretched wings alights in the upper reaches of another tree that forms the headboard of a bed *(figure 228)*. A black bear cub stood on the slope of a roof outside a window, its glass eyes gazing toward the owner's dressing table. A felt pen-wiper in the Adirondack Museum, originally belonging to Dr. Arpad Gerster's family, would be unremarkable were it not for the stuffed chipmunk curled up snugly in the center.

Taxidermy was a thriving business from 1875 to 1925, and it is easy to discern atavistic currents underlying the accumulation of stuffed wildlife in domestic interiors. Two letters in the Adirondack Museum's collection to Saranac Lake taxidermist Charles Dickert are probably typical. One asks that he make porcupine feet into two thermometers; the other, dated January 17, 1917, expresses the hope that Dickert will make an inkwell out of a moose hoof.

Furnishings made of antlers are rare in the Adirondacks.[15] Antler chandeliers at Kamp Kill Kare and in the lodge at the Kildare Club

227

Reading area with fireplace and rustic seat fashioned from the trunk of a white-birch tree, Kamp Kill Kare, Lake Kora. Other corners of this informal library space are similarly decorated with perching birds

north of Tupper Lake may be of European origin (antler decorations were used as early as 1400 in central Europe). Two chandeliers at Camp Topridge, however, are of Adirondack manufacture, constructed for Mrs. Post by local workmen from antlers of bucks killed in the vicinity of Paul Smiths, New York *(plate 8)*.

The stag mania of the early Victorian decades, inspired by the popular paintings of Sir Edwin Landseer (1802–1873) as much as anything else, gave way to bear mania by the century's end. Deer and bears were often depicted in family groups. This symbolic domesticity would have appealed to Victorians, in addition to the cuteness of the scene and the veiled assertion of male dominance. The emergence of bears as a popular subject in the decorative arts may reflect the arrival in the United States of immigrant craftsmen from central Europe, where the bear was a common motif. The Adirondack Museum owns, for example, a hat and umbrella stand portraying a mother bear standing on her hind legs at the base of a tree, looking solicitously at her cub in the branches above, and its accompanying bench with a cub supporting each end of the seat *(figures 234 and 235)*. This furniture possesses a strong Bavarian flavor, mingled with a Victorian fondness for detail and anecdote. Furniture in the Brantingham Lake house of the John Drozes also has a bear motif *(figure 232)*. The table, rocker, armchair, and settee have rails, stretchers, and legs shallow-carved in repeat clusters of oak leaves, acorns, bark, and the stump ends of cut branches—and pairs of bear cubs snuggling affectionately. A sleeping cub reclines at the joining of five stretchers underneath the circular tabletop. The oak furniture has the rectilinear form of Eastlake and Craftsman styles, and it was probably carved by machine, perhaps one of the "new wood carving machines" described in the October 13, 1894, issue of *Scientific American Supplement*, but nothing is known about its origin. The affectionate cubs appear among several designs for rustic furniture in the library of the Cooper-Hewitt Museum *(figure 233)* that were probably prepared for a line of furniture by a manufacturer in or near New York City.

Interest in bear furniture must have been brief, coinciding with the construction of those multichambered Victorian mansions in whose dim hallways an encounter between people and bears might occur. With the Colonial Revival during and after World War I, when dark woodwork and paneling yielded to bright paint, plaster, and molding, this furniture—like so much Victoriana that did not endure removal from its theatrical context—became a marooned survivor of bygone taste whose point and purpose was lost on succeeding generations.

228

Bed with bench. Made for the "Living Room Cabin," Kamp Kill Kare, Lake Kora. c. 1916–20. Peeled pole and branch, unidentified wood. The cottage may have been constructed around the famous tree bed, which reaches to the peak of the roof. See figure 129 for another view of this room

229

Hat rack. Long
Lake (?). 1890–1910.
Mosaic twig work,
three pairs of deer
antlers, 16⅛ x 30⅝".
The Adirondack
Museum. Gift of
James Emerson

230

Plaque. Ernest Stowe, Upper Saranac Lake. 1900–11. Birch bark, yellow-birch twigs, deer hooves, and looking glass, 40¼ x 36". The Adirondack Museum. Warren W. Kay Collection

231

Gunrack. Camp Uncas. Applied birch bark and deer hooves. The Adirondack Museum. Gift of the Uncas Estate

232, 233

Armchair.
American (?).
c. 1890–1910. Oak
and leather, height
37½". Found with a
second chair, settee,
and round table,
in a camp on
Brantingham Lake.
Machine-made
carvings in shallow
relief. The carved
designs are North
European in subject
and character. The
cub motif appears in
a tinted pen-and-ink
design for a tall clock
case in the library of
The Cooper-Hewitt
Museum

234, 235

Hat and umbrella stand and bench. Bavaria (?). Late nineteenth century. Wood, glass eyes: stand, height 81"; bench, height 23½". The Adirondack Museum. Gift of Frank McLaughlin

236
A stuffed squirrel
was part of the rustic
frieze that adorned
the glassed-in dining
room of the Hiram
Duryea Camp on
Blue Mountain Lake,
built c. 1890–1910.
The space, shown in
plate 28, has since
been used as a game
room for The Hedges,
a hotel

Plate 37

Rustic frieze with raccoon's head, sunporch, The Hedges. Small stuffed birds and squirrels were once integral to the rustic decor at the Duryea Camp; most have been removed because of their poor condition. The room in which this frieze appeared is shown in plate 28

Plate 38

Living room, Trophy

Lodge, Brandreth.

For a photograph of

this room taken a

century earlier, see

figure 192

Plate 39

*Showcase.
Childwold, New
York. c. 1888–1910.
Top and base
of yellow-birch
segments, height 19½".
The Adirondack
Museum. Gift in
memory of Nanette
Ehrmann. The
showcase may have
been made by Bill
Jones for Mrs. E. P.
Gale, who made the
arrangement of snow
buntings inside*

Plate 40

Fox on stand,

Camp Topridge

Plate 41

Squirrel on rustic radiator screen, Camp Topridge

Cottage and Bungalow Furniture

237 (page 238)

Camp Stott, Raquette Lake. Photograph by
Seneca Ray Stoddard, c. 1888.
Note the use of cottage furniture,
as well as the rustic lamp stand,
piano bench, and box probably
made by Joseph Bryere

238
Kitchen, camp of George J. Whelan,
Raquette Lake, c. 1925. The hickory
chair adds a note of rusticity to what
otherwise could be a tidy kitchen in a
modern home of the period

There's more hickory in the Adirondacks than you can shake a stick at, yet few hickory trees grow in the woodlands of the Adirondack Park. Tucked away in dozens of Adirondack camps and hotels are hundreds of chairs and tables manufactured between 1899 and 1940 at several factories in Indiana, where hickory trees flourished. They met the demand for sturdy outdoor furnishings for summer places throughout the country. Simple and functional, the furniture did not look as though it belonged in anything resembling a parlor, which suited the buyers just fine *(plates 43 and 44)*.

The quantity of hickory furniture imported to the Adirondacks was staggering; even today a visitor will see enough to wonder about all the pieces lost to fire and rot. Historic photographs and postcards of hotels and children's camps show dining rooms filled with hickory chairs and tables. Covewood Lodge, on Big Moose Lake, still has more than a hundred hickory chairs and tables from the 1920s. Kamp Kill Kare, perhaps the best kept of the great camps, acquired its quota of hickory at about the same time *(figure 244)*. An old-timer from Old Forge, New York, between the outside world and the resorts in the Adirondack interior, recalls boxcars of hickory furniture arriving by rail at nearby Thendara, bound for hotels and camps farther east.

The person chiefly responsible for this influx of Hoosier rusticity into the Adirondacks was Edmund Llewellyn Brown (1873–1951), founder of the first and most productive of the Indiana factories that produced hickory furniture, the Old Hickory Chair Company. Brown, by way of Tennessee, Arkansas, and Alabama, settled in 1895 in Martinsville, Indiana, a small town about twenty-five miles south of Indianapolis. Hickory grew abundantly in the limestone soil of southern Indiana and was cut by farmers who sold new-growth saplings to manufacturers, such as carriage makers, in need of ample supplies of the hard, durable wood for their products.

By 1899, Brown was in the furniture business, operating seasonally as orders came in from customers. In 1901 he filed a patent for a bark-splitting machine; other patents probably were taken out as well, according to his daughter, Dr. Frances T. Brown, though these may have been in the name of his partners, Max and Eugene Shireman, who soon "froze him out." Apparently Brown had the know-how and the Shireman brothers had the cash.[1]

Born in Memphis, Brown named his company after Tennessee's famous son, Andrew Jackson. As a 1922 catalogue boasts, "The sturdiness of such able pioneers as Andrew Jackson, whose nickname 'Old Hickory' designates this distinctive furniture, is typified by its long-

Indiana Hickory

wearing qualities." To show the furniture in its proper setting, Brown built a two-story log house named High Rock outside Martinsville, which he used as a showroom for customers vacationing nearby.

To construct his furniture, Brown utilized hickory poles that had been boiled and bent into shape on patented metal frames. When dried, these pieces were fitted together into a remarkable variety of seats —armchairs, side chairs, rockers, settees, swings. Sometimes the rougher outer bark was kept on the poles *(figure 242)*, sometimes it was sanded off to expose the inner bark *(figure 246)*. Chair seats were woven from this inner bark. Strips hammered off a soaked hickory trunk were run through Brown's patented machine, which cut them to a standard width and thickness; then, wetted again, they were woven, a job mostly done by women and children.

All of the company's products were marked, usually with a brand on a rear leg or beneath a tabletop. One such mark, intended to distinguish the product from imitations, reads within an oval: OLD HICKORY / CHAIR CO / MARTINSVILLE, IND. The firm was called the Old Hickory Chair Company from 1898 to 1920, when "Furniture" replaced "Chair" in the company's name. About 1940, the company began to substitute caning and nylon webbing for bark in the backs and bottoms of chairs and, as another concession to the modern era, to streamline its designs. The company ceased making hickory furniture about 1968, following a fire, but dwindling supplies of hickory poles and splints and a shortage of people to do the weaving had already doomed the declining line.[2]

Old Hickory had its competitors. The largest was probably the Rustic Hickory Furniture Company in La Porte, Indiana, formed by E. H. Handley, which began operation in a barn in 1902. It identified its products with both a brand and paper labels. By 1933 the company was in receivership. A third company, the Indiana Hickory Furniture Company, was started by Emerson Laughner, a former employee of Old Hickory. Edmund Brown also may have been involved with this firm, which ceased operating early in the Depression. The existence of other companies is suggested by two children's seats, a chair and a rocker, at Covewood Lodge that bear paper labels on which only the words "Terre Haute, Ind." are legible *(figure 248)*.

The sturdiness and functional merits of hickory furniture were obvious, but a moral significance was also ascribed to it. Magazine writers under the intellectual spell of the Arts and Crafts Movement pushed traditional crafts and functional design; an anonymous writer even praised hickory furniture for its "personality, an air of definite sincerity."[3] The Indiana makers were well aware of fashion in furniture. For example, three small spindles are sometimes found between two top rails in the backs of hickory chairs *(figures 245 and 246)*, a motif associated with the furniture of Charles Locke Eastlake, an English designer who inveighed against Victorian fussiness. But hickory was primarily made for rough use. Hickory furniture endured better than most, but hikers exploring unoccupied Adirondack camps often find a tangle of hickory legs and rockers in a corner of a porch, stacked there in haste at summer's end. The bliss of the Adirondack summer camp is indifference, and neglect its usual consequence.

239

Chair. Old Hickory
[Chair] Company,
Martinsville,
Indiana. 1900–20.
Height 40". The
Adirondack Museum.
A similar model was
illustrated as the
"Diner" in the 1902
catalogue of the Old
Hickory Chair
Company. The label,
exposed to view,
reads: "Old Hickory"
in block letters above
an engraved head of
Andrew Jackson and
a picture of the chair

240
Rocking Chair.
Rustic Hickory
Furniture Company,
La Porte, Indiana.
Old Hickory's
catalogues of 1902
and 1922 called this a
"Ladies' Sewing
Chair" and a
"Sewing Rocker"

241
Chair. Old Hickory
Furniture Company,
Martinsville,
Indiana. 1900–20.
The company used
this chair as a
trademark in its
catalogues,
advertisements, and
labels. It was alleged
to have been inspired
by a chair at Andrew
Jackson's home in
Tennessee, and the
company named it
the Andrew Jackson
Chair. The 1902
catalogue listed it at
$2.75; by 1922 it was
$7.50, with a rocker
version costing a
dollar more

242
*Armchair. Old
Hickory Furniture
Company,
Martinsville,
Indiana. 1920–40.
Height 37¾". The
Adirondack Museum.
This model sold for
$6.50 in 1922*

243
*Armchair. Indiana
Hickory Furniture
Company, Colfax,
Indiana. Little is
known about this
company except that
it may have been
started by two men
formerly associated
with Old Hickory*

244

Veranda, Kamp Kill Kare, Lake Kora, c. 1900. The ingredients of the ideal porch are displayed here: hickory and Mottville chairs, a hammock, rustic planters filled with flowers and ferns, two hunting rifles, and what seems to be a mailbag hanging from a cedar post near the walk at left

245

Chairs. Old Hickory
Furniture Company,
Martinsville,
Indiana. 1920–40

246

Chairs. Old Hickory Furniture Company, Martinsville, Indiana. 1920–40. Height, 32". The Adirondack Museum. These "diner" chairs were priced at $4.25 each in the 1922 catalogue

247

Table. Old Hickory Chair Company, Martinsville, Indiana. 1900–20. This "Rustic 3-Leg Table" cost $5.00 in 1902. In 1922 the same oak-top table was selling for $16.00. An identical table at Hemlock Hall on Blue Mountain Lake was made by the Rustic Hickory Furniture Company, La Porte, Indiana

Child's rocking chair. Unknown manufacturer: Terre Haute, Indiana, on label. This rocker and a companion child's chair have been on the porch of Covewood Lodge on Big Moose Lake for years

COTTAGE
AND
BUNGALOW
FURNITURE
250

249

Chair. Old Hickory Furniture Company, Martinsville, Indiana. 1940s. After the war, Old Hickory introduced nylon webbing and more contemporary designs

250
Porch, Dormar
Farms, Lake Placid,
New York. 1915–25.
Note the Indiana
hickory furniture.
The yellow-birch
rocking chairs were
made by Lee
Fountain

251

Bill Isaacs with bentwood chairs.
Photograph by Fred R. Wolcott at Onondaga
Reservation near Nedrow, New York,
1902–13. Skill in fashioning useful
articles from materials found in nature
enabled some American Indians to earn
money in an unfamiliar cash economy

The two general types of rustic bentwood are fancy and Amish. Fancy bentwood chairs appeared earlier, in the mid-nineteenth century, and consisted of whiplike material, usually unbarked hickory sprouts or willow withes ingeniously bent in arcs, loops, and parabolas to form a comfortable and sturdy enclosure for the sitter. "Fancy" probably alluded to the rustic exuberance of such furniture: if one rustic loop was good, two or three were better and stronger. Most fancy bentwood was used for porch and lawn chairs; even the eclectic Victorians would have found it too aggressively rustic indoors.

A "fancy arm chair" illustrated in the 1902 catalogue of the Old Hickory Chair Company was found on the lawn of a cottage on Big Moose Lake (figure 254). The firm stated that its three fancy models—chair, rocker, and settee—were made of second-growth hickory (that is, new growth from the stump of a cut hickory) and that this limited the number of orders which the company could accept in a given season.[4] The pattern of the back, essentially hickory sprouts or "whips" in parallel threes or fours describing a variety of arcs, is typical of the fancy type. Hickory had its counterparts in chairs made from willow and rattan: "Please do not compare these pieces," admonished the Old Hickory catalogue, "with willow, cane, rush or other cheap goods, with which the market is flooded."

At their camp on Long Lake, a family found a bentwood rocking chair made from a hickory frame for strength, with willow withes arranged in a curving, concentric, heartlike design in the back (plate 42). The chair is fragile, pointing up Old Hickory's rejoinder about willow. Willow chairs were common, but there were fewer in the Adirondacks than elsewhere, in the Appalachian region, for example.[5]

"Amish" is used popularly for another type of bentwood chair that Amish craftsmen have made since the turn of the century, and perhaps as early as the 1880s. The Amish bentwood chair is a stripped-down version of the fancy, and its all-hickory frame is sufficiently strong to require less material for the backrest and seat, where strips of milled oak or ash are used. The strips are occasionally tapered at the bottom of the arched back, and offset near the top by oval strips resembling calipers (plate 48).

The origin of the Amish bentwood chair is still obscure. It is often found in Amish homes, according to Elmo and Mark Stoll, who are partly responsible for the revived manufacture of the chair among the Amish today in Pennsylvania, Ohio, and Ontario.[6] One Amish craftsman, William Miller, reported in 1980 that he had seen an Amish bentwood rocker that was a hundred years old. With his two sons, Miller

Rustic
Bentwood

began making Amish rockers in 1972 in Geauga County, Ohio, and within six years they turned out more than 1,200 chairs.[7] The Amish call the bentwood chair a "hecka schtool"; *hecka* for underbrush and *schtool* from the Pennsylvania-German dialect for the German *stuhl*, or chair.

Amish bentwood was far more sensitive to line and even to comfort than its fancy predecessors. The earliest reference to rustic bentwood found by the author is 1871, in the December issue of *American Agriculturist*, where there is a woodcut of a "Missouri Hoop-Pole Chair" *(figure 252)*. According to the article, anyone with a supply of smooth hickory saplings could easily make one. The woodcut shows a bentwood chair, sure enough, but not one in which anyone could sit securely.

252

Missouri Hoop-Pole Chair, *illustrated in an 1871 issue of* American Agriculturist

There are no superfluous elements in the Amish bentwood rocker; in its construction the parts are a visible union of function and form. The best bentwood chair is a marvel of artisanal engineering *(figure 256)*, its curves expressing pressure and counterpressure in leveraged hickory. That nails and time have long since tamed these forces in the wood hardly diminishes our appreciation and enjoyment of the chair, which still looks as though it might fly apart.[8] One consequence of its fine design is that the Amish bentwood chair is very comfortable. The rearward slope of the back is just sufficient to shift some of the sitter's weight to the small of the spine.

A chair that combines a conventional rigid frame with an arched back and seat of bentwood branches has also turned up in the Adirondacks within the last thirty years. Thomas Bissell, whose family has owned Endion since the 1890s, recalled that these chairs were purchased from Indians who brought them from Florida. The same chair, called a "Florida cypress chair," can be found at Camp Pine Knot *(figure 255 and plate 45)*.[9] Bill Smith, a basketmaker who has recently turned his hand to furniture, built a creditable copy of the chair in 1985, using cedar instead of cypress wood *(figure 298)*.

Since Native Americans excelled in constructing shelters, containers, and other useful items from trees and grasses, it is hard to believe that they had no role in the development of bentwood. A photograph of Bill Isaacs, an Indian on the Onondaga Reservation near Syracuse, New York, shows him seated in a fancy bentwood chair surrounded by about eight others in various stages of completion *(figure 251)*. A rustic recliner, the only bentwood furniture with an Adirondack provenance that the author has found, may have been made by a Native American. This speculation is based on the chair's rawhide webbing, similar to snowshoes in construction, a craft at which Indians were especially adept *(plate 46)*. Companions to the recliner are a sideboard and three chairs *(figures 56 and 57)*, the full set from a camp on Upper Saint-Regis Lake not many miles south of the Saint-Regis Indian Reservation in Hoganburg, New York. The furniture is partly made of slippery elm, a wood traditionally favored by Indians but not widely used, or found, in the Adirondacks.

254
Chair. Old Hickory
Chair Company,
Martinsville,
Indiana (?). c. 1900–
20. Hickory. In the
1902 catalogue, this
"fancy" chair sold for
$4.00. This chair,
photographed in the
yard of an
unoccupied cottage
on Big Moose Lake
in October 1973,
marked the start of
the author's search
for rustic furniture

255
Armchair.
Cypress (?).
Several of these
chairs at Camp Pine
Knot were probably
acquired after 1948.
Thomas Bissell
remembers similar
chairs that came
from Florida at
Endion on Long
Lake

256

Rocking chairs.

From among the furnishings for a

camp built in 1908–12 on Long Lake.

These chairs may be the finest of

their kind

257

Office of the Prospect House,
Blue Mountain Lake. Photograph
by Edward Bierstadt, c. 1885.
The largest and most fashionable hotel
in the central Adirondacks between
1882 and 1900, the Prospect House
furnished its lobby with Mottville
chairs and rockers

T he rococo curves of Victorian furniture had reached their exuberant peak in the early 1860s when the owner of a small factory in Mottville, New York, a village twenty miles west of Syracuse, embarked on a career of manufacturing practical seats for homes, institutions, and assembly halls.[10] F. A. Sinclair's "Common Sense" chairs, settees, and rockers were in the tradition of lathe-turned chairs: the slatted and splint-bottom chair of the seventeenth century, the Windsor chair of the eighteenth, and Shaker furniture of the nineteenth. The Sinclair chair was marked by durability, lightness of weight, and spare elegance; it could be used without apology in the home, or pressed into hardier public duty in school rooms, churches, fraternal lodges, hotel lobbies, and porches. Between about 1880 and 1930 sizable quantities of Mottville seats reached the Adirondacks, less than a hundred miles to the east. The chairs, with their distinguishing incised, black bands, are readily discernible in all kinds of Adirondack contexts: in the lobby of the fashionable Prospect House on Blue Mountain Lake *(figure 257)*; in the living room of General E. A. McAlpin's Trophy Lodge on Brandreth Lake *(figures 192 and 260)*; and in the dining room of Camp Wild Air on Upper Saint-Regis Lake, which belonged to the Ogden Reid family.

Francis A. Sinclair was born of Scottish parents in 1834 in New Hartford, New York. He was introduced to the chair-making business by the age of twelve (his 1876 catalogue says his experience in the craft went back thirty years). He had several partnerships; the *Syracuse Journal* of 1860 mentioned him with Andrew Blogett as being engaged in the manufacture of chairs, settees, and "cottage work." In 1862 he closed his factory and enlisted in the 9th New York Artillery for three years; he suffered a leg wound at Petersburg, Virginia, two years later and was discharged with the rank of captain in November 1864. The *Syracuse Journal* announced on September 5, 1865, that the "new firm" of Sinclair, Howe, and an unidentified third party ("a gallant trio of veterans who have served their country nobly") had opened a chair factory in Mottville and named it the Union Chair Works.

By 1867, Sinclair, now associated with Joseph Hubbard, had erected a three-story stone building and employed thirty-five workers to turn out a variety of furniture. Apparently this expansion was unsuccessful: by 1876 the company had discontinued all lines but chairs. Sinclair was operating on his own in the early 1870s and no other partner entered the picture until the turn of the century, when Albert J. Allen, of Skaneateles, became part or whole owner and the company's name became the Sinclair-Allen Manufacturing Company.

Mottville Chairs

Armchair and side chair. Union Chair Works, Mottville, New York. The armchair is described in the 1888 catalogue: "Nonpareil Union Arm Chair, Bamboo Turned, Double Cane Seat, Maple, $2.50." This armchair was used at Camp Wild Air in 1895 and at Trophy Lodge about ten years earlier (figure 260). The side chair, one of a set in the dining room of a Cranberry Lake camp, has plain rounds and flared posts similar to a model illustrated in an undated catalogue of the Sinclair-Allen Manufacturing Company, c. 1900–10

Whatever his partnerships, it is clear that F. A. Sinclair, as he called himself, was the driving force behind the imaginative design, quality, and marketing of the Mottville products. In the 1870s, with an eye to the sensibilities of post–Civil War America and the imminent national Centennial, he gave his chairs such names as Union, Old Puritan, Grandmother's Favorite, Quaker, and Old Point Comfort. In his 1876 catalogue he invites the buyer's attention to the merits of his Common Sense chairs: "The frames are made of hard wood, principally Maple and White Elm, carefully selected, free from knots and shakes, and thoroughly seasoned. Not *kiln-dried* which destroys the life and strength of timber. Each round and slat is driven as tight as possible . . . glued with 1-X glue and finished with coach varnish. They are not coarse and cheaply made like many Splint-Bottom Chairs in market, but are made by experienced workmen under my own supervision."[11]

Then, alluding to the problem that would plague both Gustav Stickley's Craftsman furniture and the Old Hickory Chair Company, he warned against "counterfeits" and asked buyers to look for his stamp on each chair. Sinclair guaranteed to replace or refund any unsatisfactory chair bearing this stamp.

259

Rocking chair and side chair. Union Chair
Works, Mottville, New York. Except for extra
incised bands, the side chair is the same model
as the "Cottage Chair" illustrated in the
Union Chair Works' catalogue of 1888 and
said to be "A good chair for Schools and
Lecture Rooms." It was listed in the catalogue
of c. 1900–10 as the "Parry Diner-Assembly
Chair," and examples of it were purchased for
the dining room at Camp Wild Air. The rocker,
in a mahogany rather than a natural finish,
was not illustrated in either catalogue

260

Living room, Trophy Lodge,

Brandreth Lake, c. 1890.

Note the two Mottville

rockers and wicker daybed.

The interiors of Adirondack

cottages tended to be gloomy.

One solution was to open

the room to the roof and

install additional

windows just below

the rafters

261
*Double rocking
chair. Mottville
Chair Company,
Mottville, New York*

262

Double rocking chair.

Union Chair Works, Mottville, New York.

The 1888 catalogue called this model

"Fireside Comfort," with the description,

"Double Rocker, Cane Back and Seat,

Maple, $9.00." The catalogue of c. 1900–

10 showed it without incised bands and

called it a "Double Porch Rocker,"

available in maple or oak for $7.25 and

$7.50. Figure 261 shows an imitation

by a local competitor

Counterfeits appeared as early as 1866, according to an advertisement in the *Syracuse Journal* for August 2 of that year; Sinclair's competitor may have been a former partner or workman, possibly Andrew Blogett or Joseph Hubbard. Twenty years later the Mottville Chair Works, Inc., was operating nearby, with some products that were barely distinguishable at first glance from those of the Union Chair Works. When Allen became owner of both companies after the turn of the century, the matter became moot. Allen's obituary in 1943 reported that he was president of the Mottville Chair Works and that he was seen to go to the office daily even though the factory had been closed for some years.[12] Sinclair's name continued to be used after his retirement from business (the date of his death is not known): an undated Sinclair-Allen catalogue of about 1905 to 1915 states that every chair leaving the factory "bears our brand *F. A. Sinclair, Mottville, N.Y.* stamped and finished in the wood."[13]

Sinclair's chairs were admired in their time. This was, one suspects, not solely due to his shrewd marketing, but also because they were as good as Sinclair claimed them to be. Both contemporary buyers' testimonials and an examination of the chairs today support this judgment. The chairs were widely distributed. In 1887, they were available in six major American cities, including Chicago, as well as England, India, Brazil, and Cuba.

Elizabeth Richards of Watertown, New York, was employed with her mother by the Mottville Chair Works around 1920, and she described the work in a letter to the author. She recalled working by the piece and being permitted to arrive early or late (you were "practically your own boss"), and to talk and sing while on the job.

I worked in the Mottville Chair Works when very young, during week ends and vacations. . . . When you walked in the shop the office was at the left, a few steps more and there was a time clock. From there you went up the stairs through a large room where the cane and uncaned chairs were. [In] a room off there the men re-finished the caned chairs.

The cane came in bales. We each had a machine to put our chairs, etc., on. The machine turned [the chair] around and you could cane the bottom. We had a pail to soak the cane in. We would keep one bundle in the pail so when the one hanging on the peg dried out we would roll up the dry one and change [it] with one in the pail.

We each had a high stool which we kept our wire fasteners, pinchers, caning knife & pegs on. The fasteners were used to splice cane when working. Some people could sit on the stool and cane. I never could.

There was another shop a half mile from this one. I worked there also. Very much the same. This was the Sinclair Allen chair shop. One difference was the kind of chair. Mottville [Chair Works] made a panel back with and without arms. We all liked these as we could make more money on them. [Both companies] would get orders for kitchen chairs and settees, day beds, all sorts of rockers. I have a panel back with arms that my sister and I bought [for] our father when we were twelve and fourteen. I'm now seventy-three. I recently caned it and had it refinished for $42.00. We originally paid $7.50 for it.[14]

263

Armchair. Union Chair Works, Mottville, New York. Stamped on arm: "F. A. Sinclair/Mottville, N.Y." The "Gen. Grant Dining-Room Chair" is the term for this model in the 1888 catalogue of the Union Chair Works. The price of the maple version was $3.00, the oak cost a quarter more. It was listed as the "Gen. Grant Arm Chair" in the catalogue of c. 1900–10 published by the Sinclair-Allen Manufacturing Company

264

Rocking chair.
Union Chair Works,
Mottville, New York.
Listed in the 1888
catalogue as a
"Ladies' Favorite
Sewing Rocker" and
in the later catalogue
of c. 1900–10 as a
"Ladies' Sewing
Rocker"

The relationship of the two companies and the duration of their respective operations have not been determined. Mottville chairs by both firms have been found in the Adirondacks in sufficient numbers to indicate that Mottville was an important source of furniture for the many cottages and lodges that were being built in the region from the early 1880s until the Depression. To judge by numbers alone, however, they were not as popular as Indiana hickory furniture. The Little Moose Lake lodge of the Adirondack League Club has a large quantity of Mottville chairs, and private cottages owned by club members are also furnished with them. A more specific connection developed between Mottville and the Adirondacks with the introduction of the "Adirondack Adjustable Recliner" shortly after 1900 by the Sinclair-Allen Manufacturing Company. This was used primarily at sanatoriums in the Saranac Lakes region, where patients took the fresh air reclining on porches. About 1904, A. Fortune & Company, a Saranac Lake store, began to advertise an Adirondack Recliner in the *Journal of Outdoor Life*. It may have been a Sinclair-Allen product, or perhaps one of Fortune's own making.

265

*Living room, Camp Paownyc, Fulton Chain
of Lakes, c. 1914. Paownyc, with its mill-finished
and dark-stained woods, its open spaces and
horizontal lines, was very much attuned to
the Arts and Crafts Movement*

The rise of Craftsman furniture about 1900 and its decline soon after World War I paralleled the career of the man who did the most to promote it. Gustav Stickley came from a midwestern family of furniture makers. Of six Stickley brothers, five came to be either in partnership or in competition at furniture factories in Binghamton, Fayetteville, and Eastwood, New York, and in Grand Rapids, Michigan. At the turn of the century when Gustav introduced a line of sturdy oak furniture modeled ostensibly after the simple plank furniture found at old Spanish missions in California, his brothers began producing similar furniture of their own. In an effort to protect what rapidly became a fashionable and lucrative style, he adopted and registered the trade name "Craftsman," and began to identify the products of his shop in Eastwood with Craftsman labels. He also established a monthly magazine, *The Craftsman*, which, according to Robert Judson Clark, became "a forum for views on current movements in the arts and an effective vehicle for spreading the taste for Stickley's own furniture and his ideas about architecture and even city planning."[15]

Like other successful manufacturers during that time of predatory copyists, Gustav cloaked his products in a mystique that could not be bought, stolen, or borrowed. Other companies, including those in Mottville, New York, and Martinsville, Indiana, adopted similar marketing strategies, ascribing brand-specific virtues to a product's origins and ownership. Gustav Stickley had seized the high ground with the Arts and Crafts Movement, which had begun some thirty years earlier in England as a protest against factory conditions and machine production. The intellectual foundations of the movement, advocating the revival of the craft shop, had long been laid by 1900, when Gustav exhibited the simple board furniture that soon evolved into what was called Mission furniture. His achievement was not in inventing ideas or styles, but in giving an American voice and identity to the Arts and Crafts Movement. He demonstrated, or very nearly so, that it was possible to marry the profit motive with homes and furnishings that were well made, well designed, and affordable.

Stickley's success was marked by the offices he opened in New York City in 1905 (the workshops remained upstate, in Eastwood). By 1915 he owned and occupied an office building with showrooms and a restaurant in the city and operated a model farm in nearby Morris Plains, New Jersey. He declared bankruptcy that year, continuing only to publish his *Craftsman* magazine through 1916. Whatever the reasons for his business failure, he had shown that taste and craftsmanship were achievable, and therefore viable, goals in a mass market.

Craftsman-Style Furniture

266

Adjustable convalescent chair.
George Stark's Hardware,
Saranac Lake, New York.
After 1900. Wood frame
with steel springs and
canvas-covered mattress,
length (extended) 67⅜".
The Adirondack Museum.
Convalescent chairs like this
one, from the sanitorium in
Gabriels, New York,
were manufactured
in great quantity for the
"wilderness cure"

Today the furniture of the Stickley brothers, Gustav's in particular, is coveted by collectors and dealers who pay moderate to high prices for it. Its rectilinear lines, solidity, dark stain, and conscious avoidance of decoration, except for the use of leather, round-headed tacks, and carefully wrought hardware, were very much an outgrowth of decorative tendencies dating back to the Queen Anne style in architecture and Eastlake-inspired ideas in furniture. Its critics may have contributed to its decline: one of these was Harold Donald Eberlein, who described Mission as "a veritable symphony of mud and mustard!"[16] and favored instead the Colonial Revival, a movement that shared certain values with the Craftsman style *(figure 54)*, but was finally incompatible with it.

Stickley's sanctimonious pronouncements could not have helped his cause. His productions, he said, possessed "sincerity" and "earnestness" and they embodied the "Craftsman Ideal." To cynics this seemed just another way of selling soap. George Leland Hunter wrote, in 1912, "Some of us have the wrong idea of rusticity and imagine that because Mission furniture is of simple design and construction, it is, despite its ponderosity, ideal to help one live the simple life."[17] Hunter, among others, criticized the outsized scale of the furniture. The complaint does not apply to the best Craftsman furniture, or to that produced by Gustav Stickley's brothers at the L. & J. G. Stickley Company in Fayetteville, New York. But, as Hunter implied, simplicity in itself guaranteed nothing; what emerged was a kind of stripped-down parody of Mission in the form of oak desks, chairs, and cabinets used in thousands of schools and libraries, whose hard, plain surfaces and sharp corners and edges seemed to embody the dullness of the classroom and its arbitrary authority for several generations of Americans who got their schooling between the Depression and the Kennedy era.

Craftsman furniture was purchased for cottages and hotels in the Adirondacks, though it is not clear how much. A lodge on Lake Wilbert was freshly furnished with it *(plate 50)*, as were camps on the Saranac and Fulton Chain lakes *(figures 49 and 265):* one, built about 1914, acquired its furniture from the L. & J. G. Stickley Company, one of Gustav's chief competitors *(figures 269 and 270)*. Paul Smith's hotel, probably the most fashionable one in the Adirondacks at the time, boasted in a brochure of 1903 that its newly built casino had been "furnished throughout with Mission furniture." Gustav Stickley seems to have owned land in the Adirondacks.[18] This is hardly surprising, since the timber-bearing Adirondacks were only about sixty miles east of the Craftsman workshops in Eastwood.

267

*Bench. Henry D. Swan, Wadhams, New York. 1895–
1911. Oak with ash splint woven on removable
frames, 55 x 80¼ x 32⅜". The Adirondack Museum.
Acquired from the venerable Hand House in
Elizabethtown (which owns another), the bench
arrived badly weathered. It was sanded and stained
at the Adirondack Museum and the deteriorated ash
splint seat and back were replaced in 1982 by new
ones woven by basket-maker William Smith of
Colton, New York. The bench clearly has a kinship
to the Arts and Crafts Movement. A similar bench
appears in front of Swan's shop in figure 292*

268
Morris chair. Henry
D. Swan, Wadhams,
New York. 1895–
1911. Oak with woven
ash-splint back and
seat, 46 x 34 x 36".
The Adirondack
Museum.
The chair has an
adjustable back; like
the Swan benches in
figures 267 and 292 it
reveals its Arts and
Crafts Movement
parentage

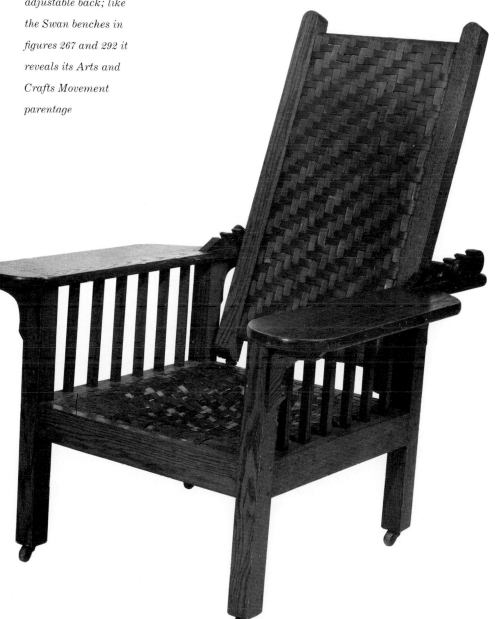

269, 270
Armchair and stool.
L. & J. G. Stickley
Company,
Fayetteville, New
York. After 1900.
Oak and leather:
armchair, height 38";
stool, height 17".
These pieces were
among the
Craftsman-style
furniture ordered for
Camp Paownyc, on
the Fulton Chain of
Lakes, c. 1914

271, 272

*Footstool. Craftsman
cabinet shops,
Eastwood, New
York. 1900–15. Oak
and leather, top 11¾
x 11¾". The
Adirondack Museum.
This footstool was
listed in the 1909
Craftsman catalogue
for $2.50. The label is
on the canvas lining
underneath the
footstool*

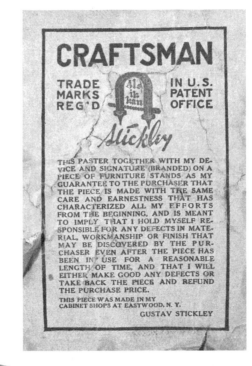

273, 274

*Stool. Keene Valley
Industries, Keene
Valley, New York. c.
1933–34. Height
17⅜". The
Adirondack Museum.
Gift of Mr. and Mrs.
Robert Worth. This
short-lived venture
was an attempt to
make work for town
residents during the
Depression*

275
Prototype of the Westport chair,
made by Thomas Lee at the
Lee family's summer home on Lake
Champlain. Westport, c. 1903

The Adirondack chair, that angular lawn classic with slatted seat and back, has only its name to connect it to the region. Its provenance remains a mystery, meaning that it is still confused with the older Westport chair, to which it bears a resemblance. The Westport chair is certifiably Adirondack, the Adirondack chair has not yet been proven to have originated in the Adirondacks *(figures 279 and 284)*.

Slat construction enabled hobbyists and local entrepreneurs to make an inexpensive lawn chair by nailing together pieces of what would otherwise have been considered scrap wood. The Adirondack chair may date from the 1920s; certainly it was common by World War II. The chair is still distributed throughout the United States, and has become an icon of the suburban and country home. However uncertain its history, the Adirondack chair on the lawn or porch became a familiar refuge on warm summer evenings.

The Westport chair, in contrast, was constructed of boards rather than slats, and it was heavier and more amply proportioned. Almost certainly it is older than the Adirondack chair; and while it was replicated outside the upstate region, its original distribution seems to have been within a hundred-mile radius from the small village of Westport, New York, on Lake Champlain, where it was manufactured from 1904 to about 1930. The Westport chair did not gain general acceptance by name; indeed, it was always known to one Westport lady as "Uncle Tom's chair." [19]

The lady in question was Mary Lee, whose family were descendants of the Lees of Colonial Massachusetts. In a letter written in 1962 to Mary Marquand Hochschild, who had inquired about the chairs found in the vicinity of Westport, Miss Lee recalled that she was a girl when her uncle enlisted the Lee clan in a chair-making project at the family's summer cottage, Stony Sides, on Westport's north shore. It was around 1900: "I can vaguely recall Uncle Tom's nailing boards together [into a chair], and getting various members of the family together to sit in it and tell him when the angles felt exactly comfortable. Then he evolved those great wide flat arms on which you set a cup or glass. Everyone was very much pleased with Uncle Tom's chair and they immediately had two or three more made by a carpenter for the piazza at Stony Sides." This was the genesis of the Westport chair.

Two of Thomas Lee's chairs were on the terrace of Stony Sides on a gray, chilly day in the summer of 1974 when Mary Lee admitted a visitor who had asked about them. Serving tea to her guest from a silver teapot, she said she did not know how the Adirondack name had

Westport and Adirondack Chairs

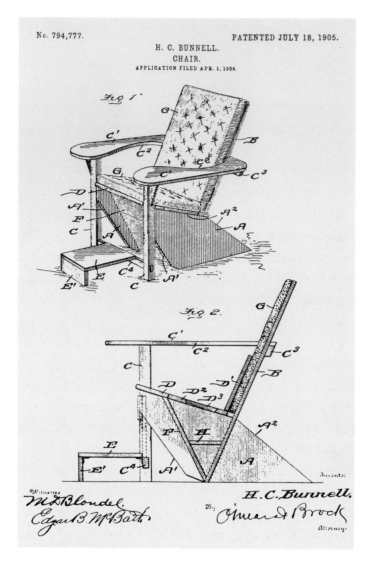

Patent for the Westport chair, July 18, 1905. The patent states: "The object of this invention is a chair of the bungalow type adapted to be converted into an invalid's chair"

become associated with the chair her uncle had invented. Westport, for one thing, was not considered to be a part of the Adirondacks when she was a girl, even though the mountains rose about ten miles to the west.

She related how her uncle's invention came to be manufactured: Thomas Lee had occasionally hunted with Harry Bunnell, a carpenter in Westport. "One time while they were shooting together," she said, "Bunnell said to Uncle Tom that he was dead broke and didn't know how he was going to get through the winter. He had a small carpentry shop in his house. Uncle Tom said to him, 'I've got a chair that I made that people seem to like very much. I'll lend it to you and you can make a few copies of it, and perhaps you can sell them.' Bunnell grabbed at the chance, borrowed the original chair, and started making them."

Bunnell filed for a patent on a version of Thomas Lee's chair on April 4, 1904 *(figure 276)*. The Lees knew nothing of this until the patent was awarded in 1905, and then they did nothing about it. The patent diagram includes a storage compartment, footrest, and cushions, additions to Thomas Lee's original design, but Bunnell does not seem to have manufactured this more elaborate chair—none, at any rate, is known today. He may have added these features to protect "his" invention. He was surely eyeing the lucrative market for convalescent furniture needed to accommodate the hundreds of tubercular patients flocking to the Adirondacks for the "wilderness cure"—weeks of quiet rest and fresh air spent on the porches of sanatoriums and cottages.

One of Bunnell's chairs that has survived was painted a red brown; others were left unpainted, like the original chairs by Thomas Lee. Hemlock, a wood not generally believed to be suitable for furniture, was used by Bunnell, as well as basswood. Bunnell's business seems to have flourished. In 1922 he introduced "improvements" to the original bungalow chair: a child's chair, a tête-à-tête *(figure 278)*, and a "convertible" chair *(figure 282)* that becomes a rocker when a board lifts and suspends the seat above curved rockers. The child's chair and the rocker are unpainted; the tête-à-tête is stained reddish brown.

The imposing form of the Westport chair is often visible in front of houses and cottages on the winding roads of Essex and Clinton counties. There are some at the Westport Country Club; a dozen scarred veterans of years of hard use survive on a broad porch overlooking a

277

The stamp that Bunnell used to identify his chairs, from the backrest of the chair in figure 279

278

Tête-à-tête chair.

Henry C. Bunnell. c.

1925. Basswood, reddish

brown stain added,

width 60½". The

Adirondack Museum.

The chair was found

in Schenectady, New

York

playing field at Camp Dudley, that oldest of boy's camps, in continuous operation since 1884. These chairs do not bear a maker's mark, but their proximity to Westport confirms authenticity.

Versions of the Westport chair have been produced outside the Adirondacks. Years ago, the Adirondack Museum made some replicas from its lone original and placed them on the museum grounds, where they aroused so much interest among visitors who wanted chairs of their own that the museum had some knocked-down replicas made in a Tupper Lake shop. Unfortunately, the chairs could not be made at a reasonable retail price, so the museum offered a measured drawing of its Westport chair for do-it-yourselfers, and over one hundred and fifty plans were sold in the first year. Anyone with basic carpentry skills and knot-free lumber can make the Westport chair; the secret, as revealed by Mary Lee, lies in getting Uncle Tom's angles "exactly comfortable."

279

Chair. Henry C. Bunnell, Westport, New York. 1905–25. Hemlock, brown paint added, height 39¼". The Adirondack Museum. Gift of Mrs. Frederick Upham

280, 281
Chair-recliner.
Raquette Lake area.
Two interlinked
planks, one cusped
and serving as a
backrest, the other
with a pair of casters
at each end and
serving as the seat,
stained brown, length
of backrest 54¼";
length of seat 67⅞";
width 17⅝".
The Adirondack
Museum. Gift of
Herbert Birrell.
Ungainly as it
appears at first
glance, this seat is
comfortable, can be
tipped from a chair
to a recliner in a
trice, and rolls
obediently on wheels
from one spot on a
porch or terrace to
another

282

Convertible chair.
Henry C. Bunnell.
After 1922.
Unpainted. Patented
July 25, 1922, "an
improvement" on the
original Westport
chair. It converts to a
rocker

283

Love seat. Unpainted oak.
Willsboro Wood Products, Willsboro,
New York. c. 1986. A variation on the
Adirondack chair

284
Chair. Unpainted
oak. Willsboro Wood
Products, Willsboro,
New York. c. 1986.
The classic
Adirondack chair is
not known to have
originated in the
Adirondacks

285
Shady Nook Inn,
Redford, N.Y., 1922.
The cast-iron bench
is similar to the
bench illustrated in
figure 19

Plate 42
Rocker. Hickory and
willow, width 23¾".
The Adirondack
Museum. Gift of the
Robert Fast Family.
The rocker is from a
camp on Long Lake

Plate 43
Dining room with
rustic work in cedar
and applied birch
bark, Loch Haven
Camp, c. 1908. The
dining table and
corner cupboard are
local, but the chairs
and screen are
Indiana hickory

Plate 44
Indiana hickory
armchairs and
planter on a dock on
Blue Mountain Lake

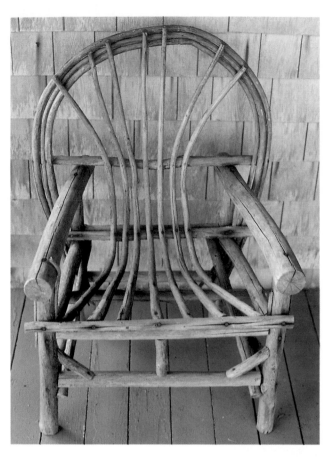

Plate 46

*Recliner. See figures
58 and 59 for
description*

Plate 45

Armchair. Cypress

Plate 47
Adirondack chairs at
Mohonk Mountain
House

Plate 48
Rocking chair.
Bedford,
Pennsylvania (?).
c. 1910. Hickory and
ash (?). This chair is
one of a pair from a
turn-of-the-century
camp on Blue
Mountain Lake

Plate 49

Rocking chair. John

Martin, Aylmer,

Ontario. 1982.

Hickory

286

At Lake George.

Photograph by

Seneca Ray

Stoddard, 1879

From Old-Time Rustic Workers to Contemporary Craftsmen

287 *(page 298)*

*A group in front of a
rustic service
building at Camp
Stott, c. 1890. Joseph
Bryere is on the left*

288
*Mr. and Mrs. Joseph
Bryere on their
wedding day, July 8,
1884. Photograph by
J. F. Holley of
Schroon Lake, New
York*

The knowledge needed for survival in the Adirondack wilds was embodied in the Adirondack guide, in whose care was placed the safety and comfort of the sportsman (occasionally a woman) during sojourns in the woods that lasted, as a rule, from one to ten days. Every aspect of the Adirondack experience, from success at finding game to setting up camp and preparing tasty meals, depended upon the skills of the guide. "If the guide possesses the usual ingenuity of his class," wrote Marc Cook in 1881, "he will be able to build tables, chairs, a lounge, and many other useful articles of furniture."[1] In the last quarter of the nineteenth century, a few Adirondack guides—the Indian Mitchell Sabattis and "Honest John" Plumley, for instance—were minor celebrities as a consequence of accounts in periodicals and books that praised their prowess and manly character. Guides universally basked in the warm light of this admiration by the public, which saw them as real-life incarnations of James Fenimore Cooper's fictional hero, Natty Bumpo.

Many of the men who made rustic furniture were Adirondack guides. Indeed, when the Adirondack Guides Association began promoting their services in March 1895 at the annual Sportsman's Show in New York City, they mounted displays of what they considered to be symbols of their profession: a guideboat, guns and fishing rods, stuffed wildlife, pelts of fur, a hut decorated with evergreen boughs, and one or two articles of rustic furniture. Attending these yearly events were as many as ten guides, each attired in a uniform consisting of a fedora, dark wool pants and jacket, a vest displaying a watch chain, and somewhere on their person, a pipe.

Like the versatile guide himself, year-round residents of the Adirondacks were forced to be jacks-of-all-trades to support themselves in a region where nearly all jobs were seasonal ones. From spring to late fall, men worked out of doors as lumberjacks, carpenters, and laborers at construction sites. These jobs might be combined with employment as guides and caretakers at camps and hotels. Wives sometimes joined their husbands; otherwise they remained with their children at what probably resembled a frontier home. A subsistence farm, this generally consisted of a plain frame house, a small barn and pasture, a kitchen garden, and some livestock, which included a cow more often than a horse, together with fowl, pigs, and perhaps sheep.

Whatever his skills and jobs, the Adirondack resident, making a virtue of necessity, devoted the snowbound months (roughly between December and the "mud season" in March and April) to tasks in the home and shop. Guideboats were fabricated in the solitude of deep

Adirondack winters: hand and mind were kept occupied, and selling one or two was not a problem—there were never enough guideboats for all who wanted to buy them.

Much of the rustic furniture illustrated on these pages was produced during the winter months. This kind of work was a specialized branch of carpentry, and not all carpenters building a camp would be equally adept at piecing together posts, branches, and bark as decoration on cottages and boathouses or designing and building rustic furniture. Architects would likely have been the first to confess their inability to give direction to the men who had these skills, since the materials with which they dealt were "undimentioned" by their very nature and therefore could not be shown with any precision on a construction plan. In any event, furniture making was not a widespread sideline among the men who did construction.

Rustic furniture making in the Adirondacks was sporadic, and its flowering took place during a relatively brief period, from 1875 to 1925. As it was largely an anonymous activity of men who worked alone, it is difficult to generalize about them. One group seems to have made furniture more as a personal indulgence than as a source of income. Another produced rustic furniture in multiples of a few designs; for these, the craft probably brought in part of a livelihood.

The most inventive work, seemingly done as whim and God allowed, was intended for particular camps, probably those where the makers had been, or were, employed. The rustic furniture at camps in and near Raquette Lake was idiosyncratic—no two pieces, except perhaps for twin beds *(figure 103 and plate 5)*, were just alike. Had production and income been foremost, then designs would have been replicated, and it is unlikely that mosaic twig work, the most difficult and time-consuming of rustic handwork, would have been tackled at all. Rustic furniture was the Adirondack male's equivalent of quilting: no one *had* to quilt, and country wisdom held activities of personal choice to be likeable by definition.

The most prolific rustic builder on Raquette Lake, and probably the most important, was Joseph Bryere (1860–1941), a Canadian who arrived on the lake in 1880 and married and settled there five years later. (See pages 307–27 for biographies of makers of rustic furniture in the Adirondacks.) A carpenter, Bryere helped build Camp Fairview in 1880–82, and with his bride was caretaker and guide at the island camp for several years *(figure 288)*. By 1887 he had moved to a similar situation at the Stott Camp on Bluff Point *(figure 287)*. The Fairview and Stott properties were among a half dozen on which family and friends of the Durant family built camps, the preeminent one being Camp Pine Knot. Bryere worked for this circle, and it is possible that the rustic furniture at the camps was made by him, though this cannot be proven. The photographer Seneca Ray Stoddard, in his guidebook *The Adirondacks, Illustrated* of 1893, called Bryere an "artist in rustic wood" whose "services in [that] particular line are at a premium in the woods," and he concluded, "Many camps hereabouts show beautiful specimens of his skill."[2] Bryere opened a hotel on Raquette Lake in 1890, and except for a clock case *(figure 224)*, all the furniture known to be by him was made for Brightside-On-Raquette. Most of this furniture was given to the Adirondack Museum by his daughter Clara Bryere. To judge from Stoddard's remark, however, other Bryere handiwork can be found elsewhere on the lake.

There were others in the vicinity capable of making fine rustic furniture. Seth Pierce (c. 1829–after 1910, *figure 289*) is the attributed maker of the corner cupboard from Camp Cedars *(figure 205)* and the giant sideboard at Trophy Lodge on Brandreth Lake *(figure 206)*. An

289

Seth Pierce with Will Kelley (left) and Ed Gilmore (right), Raquette Lake, October 1910

290–292
*Henry D. Swan, his
son Carl A. Swan,
and their cabinet
shop in Wadhams,
New York.
Photographs by C.
Underwood, c. 1890–
1900*

equally monumental sideboard, at the former Stott Camp, may also be attributed to Pierce *(figure 207)*. Another man who did rustic work, though nothing extant can be said to be by him, was Frank Fortin (born c. 1877). A newspaper item in 1900 noted that Fortin, an employee at Camp Pine Knot, had just completed a rustic scene made up of birch bark, twigs, and moss. However, he would have been too young to have produced the rustic furniture that was in place at Pine not when William West Durant sold it to Collis P. Huntington in 1895.

Few Adirondackers earned anything like a living from making furniture. Henry Bunnell, who manufactured the Westport chair for about twenty-five years, may be said to have done so, but he was not a true rustic worker. Nor was Henry Swan, perhaps the only cabinetmaker among the makers listed in this book, who with his son turned out a variety of better-quality seats and case pieces at a shop in Wadhams, New York *(figures 290–92)*. Among their products was a chair and a bench *(figures 267 and 268)* derived from the Arts and Crafts furniture designs of William Morris.

Lee Fountain (1869–1941) was one of few men who can safely be said to have earned something like a livelihood from making twiggy rustic furniture. A dozen or so chairs and several tables by him have turned up in recent years *(figures 62, 131, and 132)*. In 1921 he was reported to have been seen passing through his home town of Wells, New York, with a wagon-load of furniture he intended to sell at his store in the town of Speculator. Elmer Patterson (1859–1949), perhaps following Fountain's example, began to make yellow-birch chairs and tables in the 1920s, selling them from his family home in Speculator *(figure 67)*. According to his niece, he was not successful, and discontinued the effort after several years.

The connecting lakes in the north central part of the Adirondacks, known as the Saranacs, were developed a decade or two later than Raquette Lake. Camp construction provided employment to many artisans and businesses in and near the town of Saranac Lake. It may have been to these camp owners, some of whom were immensely rich, that D. Savage looked for buyers for his furniture. His stamp, on a desk from a camp near Tupper Lake *(figures 174 and 175)*, gives the

293, 294

Christopher "Kit"
Brown, c. 1925, and
Brown with the
chairs he made for
Mrs. Merriweather
Post at Camp
Topridge on Upper
Saint-Regis Lake

village of Saranac Lake for an address. This suggests something about his ambition to establish a business of rustic furniture manufacturing, but unfortunately nothing besides the desk and two other pieces, both unmarked, has been uncovered concerning him. Christopher "Kit" Brown made rustic furniture for Camp Hoff on Lower Saint-Regis Lake, where he was employed as a caretaker, and for nearby Camp Topridge *(figure 293)*. His chairs, somewhat rigid and rectilinear, remain at Camp Topridge, which was given to New York State by the Merriweather Post estate after Mrs. Post's death in 1974 and sold by the state to a private buyer in 1985 *(plate 6)*.

It was in the hands of Ernest Stowe that rustic furniture found its finest expression. Little is known about Stowe: a bachelor, he was a skilled carpenter much in demand at the estatelike camps being built on the Saranac Lakes around the turn of the century. He produced rustic furniture—mostly of unbarked yellow birch, whole rounds and halves, with panels of white-birch bark—at a number of these properties, according to Clarence and Bill Petty, who recalled watching him at work. Several assemblages of Stowe's furniture have turned up; one

of these, consisting of fifteen pieces including a set of six dining chairs, was given to the Adirondack Museum in 1982 by the estate of Warren W. Kay, who owned a camp on Upper Saranac Lake where Stowe lived and did most of his work. Stowe's achievement, a major one, lay in his marriage of rustic materials to high-style, classically derived cabinet forms and their proportions. In the best of his work *(figures 169–72)*, the result is both convincing and authentic; the rustic materials and the forms are integrated without impairing or compromising the nature of either. In 1911, Stowe left the Adirondacks for Florida and never returned. His life and the models for his furniture are a mystery, but his finely crafted furniture reveals a concentration of effort that seems to have been made possible by the solitude of the Adirondack wilds.

Little rustic furniture was produced between the Depression years of the thirties and the renewal of the craft starting in the early 1970s. An exception was the camp constructed for Mr. and Mrs. Walter Hochschild on Eagle Lake, near the hamlet of Blue Mountain Lake, New York, in 1937–38. Consisting of a log lodge of two-and-a-half floors, a rustic dormitory nearby with kitchenette and dining area for children and guests, and a boathouse containing space for a studio and encompassing an unobstructed view of the lake, the camp was furnished extensively with rustic chairs, sofas, tables, beds, and other furniture fashioned from peeled three- to five-inch spruce posts, after designs drawn by Kendall Rogers of Willsboro, New York *(plates 22, 23, 26, and 27)*. Not since the camps of William West Durant and his immediate successors, in the heyday years between 1895 and 1915, had there been a project of this extent and unity of design in the Adirondacks.

There was a decline in camp construction after the Depression, and World War II perpetuated the slump, as camp owners made do with the furniture they already had. If they needed a certain item, hickory furniture could be ordered from department stores or from the factory in Martinsville, Indiana. After the war tubular furniture of aluminum with seats and backs of webbed nylon tape was introduced. Changes in life-style, including inexpensive travel abroad and winter vacations in Florida and the tropics, conspired to suppress the demand for locally produced camp furniture. Americans invested their money on development houses—on recreation rooms, patios, and backyards. Some children signaled their adulthood by boycotting the old vacation camp altogether; for them the place was a painful reminder of one's dependency on others, past and present. And the air conditioner—in the office, home, even the car—nullified much of the discomfort that had sent generations of city dwellers in flight to the cooler uplands in July and August.

The arrival of Ken Heitz in the Adirondacks in 1971 may be used to mark the beginning of the revival of rustic furniture manufacture in the region. Heitz gave up a corporate job in New Jersey that year and moved with his family to a tract of wooded land east of Indian Lake, New York *(figure 295)*. He began to make rustic furniture, much of it from ironwood, and managed to earn a living from his production *(figure 296)*. In 1982 a Heitz bookcase was offered at Bloomingdale's store in New York City for the princely sum of $1,395; his chairs carried price tags of between $400 and $600 apiece. He says he has all the orders he can handle.

Another rustic worker early on the revival scene, albeit outside the Adirondacks, was Gary Shulte, an employee at Mohonk Mountain House in the Shawangunk Mountains, whose principal job from spring to early autumn is the repair and construction of cedar shelters and seats. This task, which has occupied ten of his thirty years, is a big one: Mohonk is not precisely sure how many of the picturesque contrivances it owns, except that they are in excess of a hundred. In 1976, when the author first met Shulte, he was also selling whimsical garden seats fashioned from red cedar material left over from his repair work, and he was still doing so at Mohonk in 1984, the year he completed construction of a long rustic arbor in the garden at the famous resort hotel.

During the 1970s young adults like the Heitz family continued to move into rural areas of the United States. The Adirondacks was no exception. These new settlers joined the native population in getting work where they could find it, sometimes as an employee but preferably as an independent worker answerable to no one except a customer or client. Furniture making seemed a worthwhile outlet, at least experimentally; the material was as close as the woods that can be seen from every home in the Adirondacks, the activity was unregulated, and rustic pieces could be made anywhere and virtually in any season.

Among those who hoped to make a living from rustic carpentry was Jamie Sutliff, who had been raised near the Adirondacks and moved there after an itinerant period that included folk singing and working on a ranch in Colorado. Sutliff experimented with wood carving, his preference, but he also tried his hand at making a variety of furniture —some rustic, some not—in the barn he had converted to a house in Long Lake, New York *(figure 297)*. Barry Gregson is a stonemason

295, 296
Ken Heitz, Indian
Lake, New York, and
an ironwood bench
by Heitz

297

*Chairs. Jamie
Sutliff, Long Lake,
New York. Ash*

who produces Christmas wreaths, ax handles, mauls, and carpenter's planes during the winter months. Seeing an opportunity, he began to make rustic furniture that he sold to the owners of the camps where he was working *(plate 20)*. A log house at the North Woods Club, newly finished in 1985, contains some rustic furniture by Gregson, who lives in nearby Schroon Lake, New York. Bill Smith, also a north-country native, supplements his successful basket-making business, a craft he learned from Indians as a boy, with furniture making. Smith fashions rustic stands and benches at his residence in Colton, in the northern Adirondacks *(figure 298)*. Thomas Phillips of Tupper Lake, New York, restores rustic furniture as well as making it.

Contemporary rustic work has not been confined to the country. Dan Mack, formerly a broadcast journalist, makes rustic beds, chairs, tables, stands, and ladders of maple and beech at a studio in Harlem in New York City *(figure 299)*. Peter Read, perhaps the only contemporary rustic worker trained as a cabinetmaker, constructed a high chest at his Manhattan shop, in 1982, using birch bark gathered at his family's camp near Tupper Lake, New York *(figure 300)*. Names in the New York Yellow Pages, such as Treetop Company, Impressions in Wood, and One-of-a-Kind, suggest the market that exists for rustic relief in the city; in addition, they reflect an attitude, altogether new to the craft, that admires the furniture as much for its artistic qualities as for its utility.

Factory-produced rustic furniture, of the sort that had not been available for a generation or two, now finds buyers who know little or nothing of its earlier incarnations. Mail-order catalogues and department stores advertise this furniture. There are willow chairs from shops in North Carolina, Kentucky, and Arkansas, and cypress seats from Florida. Amish craftsmen in Ohio, Pennsylvania, Tennessee, New York, and Ontario sell rockers and other furniture of bentwood hickory.

298
William Smith,
Colton, New York, in
his cedar copy of a
Florida cypress chair

One rocker sold for $135 in 1983, surely one of the best bargains obtainable *(plate 49)*. Also reasonably priced is the Adirondack chair *(figure 284)*, which has been sold for years, assembled and in kit form, at the Adirondack Store in Lake Placid, New York. The chair is manufactured at a half-dozen shops elsewhere as well, including the Willsboro Wood Products Company, in Willsboro, New York. A Beverly Hills, California, company in 1985 announced itself "manufacturers of new age Adirondack furniture" in a promotional flyer illustrating an Adirondack chair and carrying the headline "California Adirondack." And Walpole Woodworkers of Walpole, Massachusetts—as it has been doing, unher-

300

Cabinet. Peter Read,
New York City. 1982.
Birches at his
family's camp near
Tupper Lake
supplied Read with
bark for the base

alded, for years—continues to produce homely cedar deck furniture reminiscent of the 1950s. It has the redeeming virtue of comfort, durability, moderate price, and a refreshing lack of pretense. Hickory furniture production was resumed in Indiana in 1982, a development made possible largely because rustic furniture had become fashionable again. Taking the Old Hickory Furniture Company's name, the new owner began operations in Shelbyville, Indiana, and issued a catalogue, the first in perhaps twenty-five years.

Just where this appetite for rusticity will lead is anybody's guess. Tried and tested rustic furniture, such as that produced in factories and shops over a long period of time, should succeed as long as consumers find natural materials a consoling relief from the artificial stuff that makes up so much of the environment where they live and work.

Twiggy furniture, on the other hand, of the kind made in the Adirondacks, and illustrated in these pages, remains a cottage industry. A recent exception is Grant's Adirondack Furniture Company, which started operating in 1985 with four men at a small factory in Saranac Lake and an office in Lake Placid. Supplying designers and architects, the firm ships almost all of its twiggy production outside the Adirondacks. Rustic furniture, however, will be subject to the vagaries of the economy—but then this is nothing new to craftspeople who know firsthand the difficulties of living by one's own wits and cunning. It seems to the author that the potential of contemporary rustic work remains largely unexplored. Today's workers so far have confined themselves mostly to sticks and posts. As this is being written, however, there are signs of a more venturesome spirit: mosaic twig work and applied bark have begun to appear on the smaller items of one or two craftsmen. This experimentation, which is, after all, what their predecessors on Raquette Lake and elsewhere in the Adirondacks were occupied with a century earlier, should be continued and encouraged.

Related to this is another circumstance: no one knows much about rustic materials and how they behave or age over time. There is no "rustic craft" in the sense that cabinetwork is based on centuries of transmitted experience. There have been no apprentices to a master rustic worker—at least not to the author's knowledge. Lack of a strong tradition may encourage the untalented to try a hand at rustic work, and the poor quality of the resulting product may do harm to the future of a craft in its infancy. It would be helpful if rustic workers shared their hard-won knowledge with one another, not simply because it would sharpen and broaden their skills, but because it might also improve their standing among those whose opinions count—the buyers and those discriminating seekers of the durably Good, the connoisseurs.

This book can be reckoned a success if it imparts to the reader an appreciation of a little known craft practiced by Adirondack woodsmen a century or so ago. But its usefulness will be still greater if from its examples and illustrations artists today discern that the creative uses of root and branch, of bark and twig, have barely been explored. They must heed the trees and shrubs whispering outside their houses and scratching at their windows.

301
John Champney on a
dock at Tupper Lake,
1913

ALGER, FRANK (c. 1875–after 1940): Alger *(figure 302)* made four cedar stands for the Eagle Nest home of Captain and Mrs. Boris Sergievsky at Blue Mountain Lake, New York. He was a caretaker and housepainter at the estate from 1912 to 1920, and superintendent by 1938. According to *The History of Hamilton County*, Alger was known as a painter in Indian Lake by 1925, and called "the Indian." *(See figures 118–20.)*

ASHER, JOSEPH (fl. 1900): Asher was employed at W. W. Durant's Blue Mountain and Raquette Lake Steamboat Line. Listed in 1900–1 as "head ship carpenter," he probably worked on Durant's steamboat *Tuscarora*, which was launched on Blue Mountain Lake in 1900 and is beached there today. Under the top of a small pedestal table found in the attic of an old store in Blue Mountain Lake is the inscription "Joe Asher/April the/5 1902." *(See figure 195.)*

302

Frank Alger, 1940

Rustic Furniture Makers in the Adirondacks

AUGUSTINE & SEILER: The following notice was printed in the April 24, 1879, issue of the *Boonville Herald:* "Rustic work—Messers Augustine & Seiler have removed from Delta, and opened rooms in the Jones Block, Park Row, for the manufacture of various kinds of rustic work, such as chairs, flower-stands, baskets and many other ornamental and useful articles."

BLISS, GEORGE (d. 1954) and ARTHUR (d. 1960): According to their nephew Jim Littlejohn, the Bliss brothers worked in the Lake Placid area making "seats in the woods out of tree trunks . . . also camps, furniture and railings along paths, rustic stuff," some of yellow birch.

BROWN, CHRISTOPHER "KIT" (fl. 1920–30): Brown made rustic furniture for E. A. Hoffman's Camp Hoff on Lower St. Regis Lake, according to his son, James C. Brown, who by 1975 had himself been employed at the camp for forty-seven years.

"Kit" also produced rustic furniture for Mrs. Merriweather Post at nearby Camp Topridge in the 1920s. *(see figure 294 and plate 6.)*

BRYERE, JOSEPH O. A. (1860–1941): Bryere *(figure 288)* was the most productive rustic craftsman on Raquette Lake and vicinity and probably also the most important and influential. The Glens Falls photographer, Seneca Ray Stoddard, referred to Bryere as "an artist in rustic wood," and noted in the 1892 edition of his *The Adirondacks, Illustrated* that, "His services in this particular line are at a premium in the woods and many camps hereabout show beautiful specimens of his skill."

According to Clara O. Bryere, her father was born in Quebec and first visited Raquette Lake in 1880 or 1881. He married and settled there several years later. Charles Durant employed him as a carpenter and caretaker at Camp Fairview in 1883–86, after which he worked with his wife at the Stott family's camp on Bluff Point until 1890 *(figure 287)*. During the late 1880s he began building a hotel on the lake, called "Brightside-On-Raquette," which opened for business in 1890. His daughter described him as a guide, camp builder, and carpenter, who sometimes turned his attention to making furniture in the winter. She gave eleven pieces of his handiwork to the Adirondack Museum in 1957 and 1974. An acquaintance in his eighties recalled Bryere's fondness for wearing flashy clothes on visits to Utica; Bryere wore a top hat in the city, he said, but kept it in a box when he boarded the train in Raquette Lake so his neighbors in town would not see that he owned one. *(See figures 74, 101, 133, 165, 166, 178, 180, 186, and 224.)*

BULLARD, CHARLES E.: Glens Falls, New York. "Furniture and bedding for lake side use." *(Lake George Mirror, June 25, 1892.)*

RUSTIC
FURNITURE
MAKERS
IN THE
ADIRONDACKS
318

303
Reuben Cary,
1890–1900

BUNNELL, HARRY C.: About 1904, Bunnell began manufacturing a porch and lawn chair with raked back and seat and wide horizontal arms in a shop behind his home in Westport, New York. For over twenty years he produced at least four versions of the chair, obtaining patents on them as he had done for the original chair. The chair, known in the region as the Westport chair, should not be confused with the slatted Adirondack chair, which is a later development, possibly inspired in some way by Westport examples. Bunnell stamped his chairs. *(See figures 275–79 and 282.)*

CARY, REUBEN (1845–c. 1933): Reuben Cary *(figures 32 and 303)* was born about the time his father, Thomas R. Cary, came to the Adirondacks from Vermont. The family lived in Indian Lake and Long Lake, possibly after Thomas had sold or relinquished a camp on Beach's Lake that became part of Brandreth Park in 1851. Cary would have known Benjamin Brandreth from childhood. He guided for the Brandreths and was hired in 1880 as gamekeeper and caretaker of their preserve, which then included several large cottages and service buildings or dependencies. A carpenter and builder of guideboats, Cary was profiled in June of 1914, in a two-part article in *Forest and Stream*, entitled "Reuben Cary—Forest Patriarch." In 1874, Brandreth, a businessman and pill maker, ordered forty-eight chairs from Cary, but later he complained about poor business conditions in New York City and asked Reuben to reduce his order by half. Two chairs in the set—vernacular slat-backs with plain turned posts and splint bottoms—were given to the Adirondack Museum by Franklin Brandreth in 1976. Several of the chairs appear on the porch of Camp Good Enough in an early photograph, and Brandreth descendants believe that some rustic furniture in the cottages at Brandreth Park today was made by Reuben Cary. *(See figure 304.)*

RUSTIC
FURNITURE
MAKERS
IN THE
ADIRONDACKS
319

304

Armchair. Reuben Cary, Camp Good Enough, Brandreth Park. 1875. Sugar maple, with seat of woven caning, height 37". The Adirondack Museum. Gift of Franklin Brandreth

Table. John
Champney, West
Parishville, New
York. c. 1910–20.
Marquetry veneer,
height 26½". The
Adirondack Museum.
Gift of Mrs.
Marjorie C. Frost
and Mrs. Mary F.
Lawton in memory
of Austin M. Frost.
There is a mate to
this table; both were
originally owned by
Burt Alvord of
Saranac Lake

RUSTIC
FURNITURE
MAKERS
IN THE
ADIRONDACKS
320

CHAMPNEY, JOHN (fl. c. 1913): John Champney made a marquetry table that was given to the Adirondack Museum in 1980 by Mrs. Marjorie C. Frost and Mrs. Mary F. Lawton. According to his daughter, Champney had lived in West Parishville, just outside the northwestern border of Adirondack Park, and was "a first-class carpenter who worked on many buildings in this [Parishville] area and around Colton, Moody and Tupper Lake." He was a guide and caretaker from about 1912 to 1917 for Mrs. John Sprague, who owned a camp near Moody, New York. A photograph taken in 1913 shows him on a dock at Tupper Lake with two chairs and two chests made of yellow birch *(figure 301)*.

Regarding the table and a mate, both originally owned by Burt Alvord in Saranac Lake, Champney's daughter recalled in a letter of July 14, 1982 at the Adirondack Museum:

Down home he had a shop where he made these tables. It was not equipped with electricity. He had many expensive hand tools and a saw rig operated by a manual foot pedal. He drew his own patterns, cut strips of many kinds of natural woods (no veneer, synthetic wood), glued them together in light and dark strips in such a way that when cut with the aid of a miter box it produced very pretty designs which he laid out on a table base and glued down, forming the beautiful symmetrical designs in table tops. He did not confine himself to tables, however. He made cabinets, chests of drawers and gun stocks. For the farmers in the neighborhood he made axe helves, sled platforms, forward bobbies [runners or "bobs" for logging sleds], wagon tongues, and last but not least, he was the best saw filer for miles around.

Champney's son Herbert, now deceased, followed in his father's footsteps. He was a watchman for twenty years at the Rockefeller Preserve, west of Paul Smiths, New York. *(See figure 305.)*

COLTON, C. W.: The *Boonville Herald* for June 23, 1887, said that "many area camps" had been furnished with furniture purchased from C. W. Colton of Boonville, New York.

DUNN, NELSON (fl. 1910–30): Of Eagle Bay, Dunn was the maker of a sidetable and chest of drawers having sides of small cedar shingles in a pattern similar to the siding of the cottage where the furniture was placed, the summer home of Charles E. Snyder on Cascade Lake. *(See figure 160.)*

FISHER, ANDREW (d. 1918): An important mosaic twig sideboard by Fisher has been at Endion on Long Lake since about 1890–95, according to Thomas Bissell, whose family has owned the property since the late nineteenth century. Fisher was a guide and carpenter in the Long Lake township; he worked at the Bissell place, which later became a hotel, and he helped to build the steamboat *Glide* on Long Lake. Kenneth Durant has suggested that Fisher, not Seth Pierce, made the corner cupboard *(figure 205)* now at the Adirondack Museum. *(See figures 209 and 210.)*

FORTIN, FRANK (b. c. 1877): Two items in the *Warrensburg News* for 1900 refer to Fortin, who seems to have worked as a carpenter at camps on Raquette Lake in the last years of the century. The May 24 issue reported: "Frank Fortin has just finished one of the finest pieces of rustic work that ever has been seen in this country. The scene represents a hunter in the act of shooting. The picture is composed of birch bark, twigs and moss as they grew in natural colors. It is now at Camp Pine Knot, and is pronounced by skilled workmen to be the finest thing of its kind ever produced." Another reference, in the August 30 issue, states that Fortin's rustic picture had been a major attraction at the tenth annual fair and festival held at St. Williams Church on Raquette Lake on August 21. Collis P. Huntington, who had died at Pine Knot earlier that month, was quoted as having remarked "that it was the work of genius. . . . We have nothing like it in any of our art galleries or museums." Fortin was reported to be twenty-three years old at the time. He did some work for Dr. Arpad Gerster, who referred in an entry in his journal for September 10, 1897, to a shelf which Fortin had built in a camp previously owned by the Gerster family, next door to Camp Pine Knot. No known work by Fortin survives.

FOUNTAIN, LEE (1869–1941): Fountain, who may have produced rustic furniture longer and more systematically than any other man in the Adirondacks, was making chairs as early as 1914 and as late as 1930. Oliver H. Whitman's journal, in the entry dated September 8, 1914, notes: "Made splints for Lee Fountain 2000 . . . Lee Fountain came up hear [*sic*] and got me to make a lot of splints to bottom chairs . . . He paid me 8 dollars for two thousand splints." Whitman sold many more splints to Fountain between then and mid-April of the following year. On December 28, 1916, Whitman wrote: "I took a lot of birch stumps to Lake Pleasant

RUSTIC
FURNITURE
MAKERS
IN THE
ADIRONDACKS

321

to Lee Fountain to make tables." Four tables with root bases by Fountain are said to have survived. One of these may be the table with inlaid top purchased from the exhibition of rustic furniture held in Lake Placid in 1982 *(figure 130)*. An item in the August 1921 *Hamilton County News*, brought to this writer's attention by Ted Aber, states: "Lee Fountain passed through Wells on Saturday, August 20, with a load of furniture, his own make, which he placed on sale at Speculator." Aber also provided Fountain's funeral announcement, which said he was born in Wells, operated a hotel in nearby Speculator "for a number of years," and that "several years [ago?] he purchased and since has conducted the hunting camp at West River known as the White House." Aber and Stella King, in *The History of Hamilton County* (1965), stated that Speculator had but two stores in 1905 and that one of these was run by Lee Fountain, "whose parquet-topped tables with gnarled wooden legs are still to be seen in the older summer homes." Fountain's ledger of general store accounts, for 1905, is in the library at the Adirondack Museum. An article about Fountain appeared in the August 1983 issue of the magazine *Adirondac*, with illustrations of eight pieces of rustic furniture attributed to him. *(See figures 60, 62, and 130–32.)*

RUSTIC

FURNITURE

MAKERS

IN THE

ADIRONDACKS

322

FULLER, ABE: Four rustic chairs by Fuller are owned by the Lake Placid–North Elba Historical Society in Lake Placid, New York. *(See figures 90 and 91.)*

GUILLAUME, F. L.: An advertisement in the *Boonville Herald* for December 14, 1876, said that he was selling "rustic motto frames" for twenty-five cents each.

HAYNOR, JAKE (fl. 1900–1910): Haynor was the builder of a cottage on the west end of Goff Island on Seventh Lake in 1904, according to information given by George VanGorder. Mr. VanGorder also said that Haynor, who lived in the region of Sixth and Seventh lakes, made benches and tables for that cottage. *(See figures 107 and 108.)*

JAQUES, ALBERT and GILBERT: A photograph *(figure 92)* shows Albert Jaques making cedar furniture in Keene Valley, together with Perry Sleeper and Warren Webb. His nephew, Gilbert Jaques, also of Keene Valley, began to make rustic furniture in January 1983. *(See figure 306 and plates 13 and 14.)*

JONES, BILL (fl. c. 1890–after 1904): Earl H. Gale recalled Jones: "I saw him often at his workshop at Childwold Park on Lake Massawepie between the years 1897 and 1904. Mr. Jones had created much rustic furniture for what was then known as Childwold Park Hotel." Jones did the rustic trim shown in a photograph of an interior at the hotel taken by Seneca Ray Stoddard, and his rustic furnishings were also installed in three cottages attached to the hotel. Three pieces of rustic furniture belonging to Jean LeCompe were identified by Mr. Gale as Jones's handiwork in 1975. *(See figure 75 and plate 39.)*

PATTERSON, ELMER (1859–1949): Mrs. Clarice Stanyon, a niece of Elmer Patterson, said that he was born in Amboy, New York, west of Syracuse, and that his childhood was spent in Lewis County. In 1885 he arrived in what is now Speculator

RUSTIC
FURNITURE
MAKERS
IN THE
ADIRONDACKS
323

and began to manufacture snowshoes and pack baskets with his father, and to buy and sell parcels of property. He moved briefly to the State of Nevada, and then to Ilion, New York, where he was employed at Remington Arms during World War I. In the 1920s he began to make rustic furniture at his home in Osceola, New York, finding the locale to be more abundant in the yellow birch he needed for the furniture. He tried to sell his furniture to summer residents and tourists in Speculator without much success. Mrs. Stanyon owned eight of her uncle's pieces in 1983: several tables and rockers, and a wall stand and settee, all of yellow birch. A table was exhibited at the Adirondack Museum in 1976 *(figure 67)*, and a similar one was purchased from the rustic furniture exhibition in Lake Placid in 1982. A table found recently in Osceola bears Patterson's initials, E.E.P., and the date 1932. *(See figure 67.)*

PIERCE, SETH (c. 1829–after 1910): Pierce's skill as a carpenter and rustic worker has been confirmed separately by several oldtimers whose personal recollections of Raquette Lake date as far back as the late 1800s. In 1906, Pierce *(figure 289)* said he had known Raquette Lake for fifty-five of his seventy-seven years, though he had been a resident there only for the last thirty-eight years. "My occupation," he said, "is guiding, fishing and hunting, and once in a while I take my tools and go at carpenter work." He added that he had been a blacksmith in Blue Mountain Lake and that he helped to build Charles Durant's Camp Fairview on Raquette Lake in the early 1880s. Reuben Mick thought that Pierce had originally come from Fort Ann, and that he had also worked on Camp Cedars for Frederick Clark Durant on Forked Lake. The mosaic twig corner cupboard given to the Adirondack Museum by F. C. Durant, Jr., is attributed to Pierce, although Andrew Fisher, who also worked for the Durants, may have made it. In 1977, Franklin Brandreth reported that Frank Cary, then eighty-seven, had told him "that the sideboard in Trophy Lodge was made by a chap named Seth Pierce, who came from Long Lake and who spent a few summers at Brandreth working for Gen. E. A. McAlpin." *(See figures 205 and 206.)*

PLUMLEY, JOHN (1827–1900): Plumley was a guide for William H. H. "Adirondack" Murray in the late 1860s and assisted shortly after in building Benjamin Brandreth's cottage on Brandreth Lake. With Reuben Cary, he is a candidate for being the maker of rustic furniture at Brandreth Park, though there is no proof that he actually did so. Plumley lived in Long Lake but, according to testimony in 1906, his family often did not see him between May and October while he was picking up jobs on Raquette Lake, where he had his own camp. Murray, who wrote *Adventures in the Wilderness* (1869), eulogized "Honest John" Plumley in 1901 in the summer issue of *Woods and Waters* magazine.

RUSTIC

FURNITURE

MAKERS

IN THE

ADIRONDACKS

324

PORTER, LEWIS H. (c. 1880s–c. 1965): Porter lived in Inlet, New York, and was said by Mr. George VanGorder to have made rustic furniture. A burl top table with root base is by him, according to its owner, Ann Talmage. *(See figure 127.)*

RECTOR, EARL (fl. 1925–35?): A carpenter, he worked for Earl Covey, owner of Covewood Lodge on Big Moose Lake. Some of the rustic furniture there was made by Rector, according to Covey's widow. *(See figure 68.)*

SAVAGE, D.: His name is stamped in ink on the drawer of a birch bark desk given to the Adirondack Museum by the International Paper Company in 1979. A sideboard and buffet from the same Bog River camp are also attributed to him. *(See figures 173–76.)*

SLEEPER, PERRY (fl. 1900–20?): A summer cottage built in Keene Valley in 1913 contains furniture made by Perry Sleeper, including eight dining room chairs on which designs in the Art Nouveau Style were burned and painted by a guest from Princeton, New Jersey. Charles N. Holt says in the 1975 booklet *Adirondack Frontier* that Sleeper was one of the early cabinetmakers in Keene Valley. Sleeper also produced rustic furniture. A photograph *(figure 92)* taken about 1915 shows him with Albert Jaques and Warren Webb at a bench outdoors, surrounded by cedar seats in various stages of completion.

SNYDER, OLE LYNN (1852–1929): A lawyer from Buffalo and the first secretary, in 1890–91, of the Adirondack League Club, Ole Lynn Snyder made rustic furniture for the cottage designed and built for him in 1890 on Lake Honnedaga by William Wicks, a friend of Snyder's and author of the influential *Log Cabins and Cottages* (1889). In 1980 the cottage and its contents were destroyed by fire. Snyder's daughter, Mrs. Frederick C. Squier, stated that he made the furniture between about 1895 and 1914, and that much of the outdoor rustic work had "rotted out very fast" and was all gone by 1925. *(See figures 54, 55, 140, and 158.)*

ST. JOHN, HARMON: "A rustic sofa and rocking chair, made from the roots of pine stumps, the work of Harmon St. John, of Luzerne, were novelties in their line." An item about the 1858 Warren County Fair in *Transactions of the N.Y. State Agricultural Society* (Albany, 1859), found by H. J. Swinney.

STARKS, GEORGE L., & COMPANY: A convalescent chair at the Adirondack Museum bears the metal tag of this manufacturer in Saranac Lake, New York. In 1902, Starks's firm, then known as the Adirondack Hardware Company, was recommended to Mrs. T. M. Carnegie on the basis of construction work at Sagamore Lodge and Camp Uncas. Rustic detailing and furniture may have been a part of these jobs. *(See figure 266.)*

STOWE, ERNEST (fl. 1890s?–1911): Information about Stowe came from Clarence Petty and his brother, the late William Petty; both were raised on Upper Saranac Lake, near the cabin that Stowe occupied on property that belonged to a popular, old hotel named Corey's (later the Rustic Lodge) on Indian Carry, at the southern end of the lake. In 1911 Stowe moved to Florida, leaving his nine-by-twelve-foot cabin and carpentry tools in the care of the Petty family. He never returned, notifying the Pettys that his few belongings were theirs to keep. His cabin was skidded across the ice to the Petty place, where it remains to this day, in understandably poor condition.

A skilled carpenter whose specialty was rustic work, Stowe readily found employment on Upper Saranac Lake where a number of elaborate camps were constructed between the 1890s and World War I. The young Petty boys watched him at work in the spring of 1909 or 1910 at Isaac Seligman's Fish Rock Camp and Otto Kahn's Bull Point Camp. He helped construct camp buildings, and made rustic furniture. A bachelor, he had a retiring personality. He may have hailed from Colton, New York, a small community some sixty miles to the north of Upper Saranac Lake.

Stowe produced a quantity—large by comparison with other rustic workers in the Adirondacks—of rustic furniture characterized by close attention to detail and an adaptation of rustic materials to forms derived from traditional cabinetwork. On most of his furniture he used white-birch bark and yellow-birch rounds, though for a set of chairs and the legs of a desk he used unbarked cedar *(plate 35)*.

There are two principal collections of Stowe furniture. In addition, a half-dozen pieces were sold by the Lake Placid dealer, Robert Doyle, who could not name the camps in which they were found *(plate 32)*. The first collection, a set of fifteen pieces of Stowe furniture, including six dining chairs, was given to the Adirondack Museum in 1982 and came from the estate of Warren W. Kay. This furniture probably belonged to Isaac Simonin, said to have been in the vegetable-oil business in Philadelphia, and it was installed at Camp Ninomis (the family name spelled backward) on Second Stony Creek Pond, a couple of miles from Stowe's cabin at Rustic Lodge. Leon Shova, now retired in Tupper Lake, remembers moving the furniture in 1936 to a camp that belonged to Eugene Simonin, one of Isaac Simonin's sons. This camp, successively called Camp Arokortu ("a rock or two") and Camp West Wind, was purchased by Kay from Eugene Simonin's widow in 1957–58.

RUSTIC
FURNITURE
MAKERS
IN THE
ADIRONDACKS
325

The other assemblage of Stowe furniture, consisting of a sideboard, secretary, two chests of drawers with mirrors, table, yellow-birch armchair, and nine cedar dining chairs, is in an old camp in Hamilton County. A present owner of the camp is certain that the furniture was already there when her grandfather bought the camp in 1931. How the furniture came to be sixty miles south of Saranac Lake is a mystery. The property had previously changed hands three times, in 1895, 1901, and 1913, and the furniture was probably originally intended for a camp in the Saranac Lakes district where Stowe lived and worked. *(See figures 65, 66, 69, 167, 185, 230, plates 17–19, and 32–35.)*

SUMNER, CHARLES (c. 1861–1937): His obituary, in the *Hamilton County News* for April 1937, reported: "A carpenter, his specialty was rustic work, and much of his work was done on the estates in Long Lake, Blue Mountain Lake, and Raquette Lake." A cedar bench displayed in Lake Placid in 1982 was said to have had a label under the seat bearing the name "Sumner."

SWAN, HENRY D. (1819–1911): Of Scottish ancestry, Swan was listed in the censuses of 1880 and 1890 as a resident of the towns of Essex and Westport respectively. A notice in the March 19, 1891, issue of the *Essex County Republican*, discovered by Mrs. Ethel Kozma, reported that Swan was "still" shipping furniture "of all kinds" to New York City, Boston, and other points, and that his specialty was heavy oak chairs and "spring settles." Datelined Wadhams, New York, the item suggests that he had been producing furniture in Essex and Westport before moving to Wadhams, also in Essex County, in about 1890. A photograph of Swan's shop, which he and his son Carl A. Swan built in 1892–93 *(figure 292)*, reveals that the two made chairs and tables in a variety of styles, including a bench inspired by the Arts and Crafts Movement and a side chair with a pierced Chippendale splat of the type found in rural areas of western New England after 1790. *(See figures 267 and 268.)*

TURNER, WALTER (fl. 1909–27?): Turner was a good carpenter and "rustic man," according to Arthur Gates. Paul Maloney said that Turner worked in 1909 on his parents' camp, Minnewawa, on Blue Mountain Lake, and that he added a rustic porch to it in 1918. A cedar desk at Minnewawa is said by Mr. Maloney to have been made by Turner. A similar desk, in Camp Windy Barn, where Turner did some work about 1927, can also be attributed to him. *(See figure 100.)*

WEBB, WARREN: Of Keene Valley, he appears in an outdoor scene *(figure 92)* with Albert Jaques and Perry Sleeper working on cedar furniture.

WESTCOTT, CHAUNCEY "CHAN" (1874–1931): The camp on Buck Island, Cranberry Lake, contains rustic birch furniture said by Mrs. Richard Martin to have been made by Chan Westcott for her grandfather, Judge Irving D. Vann. An essay in the book *Cranberry Lake* (1968), in which Westcott's picture appears *(figure 307)*, describes him as a "hunter, guide and early settler."

RUSTIC
FURNITURE
MAKERS
IN THE
ADIRONDACKS
326

307

Chauncey "Chan"
Westcott, c. 1900 (?)

RUSTIC

FURNITURE

MAKERS

IN THE

ADIRONDACKS

327

WIGHTMAN, REV. PERCY: Rev. Percy made the lectern, pulpit, and communion table in the Community Chapel at Big Moose, New York, in 1938.

WILSON, GEORGE (fl. c. 1910–25?): A postcard in a picture album of the John Collins family, at Blue Mountain Lake, shows George Wilson at work on a rustic table; nearby is a mosaic twig desk *(figure 197)*. John and Pat Collins remembered Wilson but did not know much about him except that he worked as a gardener at Sagamore Lodge, near Raquette Lake. A note at the Adirondack Museum identifies him as working at the Lake View Lodge in Big Moose, New York. None of his furniture is known to have survived.

YOUNG, WILL (fl. 1905–1920): In the Stedman Collection at the Center for Music, Drama and Art, Lake Placid, are photographs taken by Irving Stedman about 1915–17, including four studio photographs of rustic furniture identified as "Will Youngs [*sic*] Furniture." The Lake Placid–North Elba Historical Society owns yellow-birch furniture that is attributed to Will Young and dated 1906. *(See figures 70, 72, 73, and 93.)*

INTRODUCTION

1. Many articles on the use of rustic furniture in contemporary interior decoration have appeared in magazines and newspapers over the past decade, signaling a renewed interest in the subject. See, for example, Rita Reif, "Logs: 'Healthy Kind of Chic,' " *The New York Times*, 9 July 1974; Harriet Heyman, "Furniture of Natural Wood," *The New York Times*, 8 September 1975; Shirley van Zante and Denise L. Caringer, "Decorating with the New Naturals," *Better Homes and Gardens*, May 1981; Marilyn Bethany, "Barking Up the Right Tree," *The New York Times Magazine*, 20 June 1982; Kimberly Goad, "Adirondack Camp Furniture," *Texas Homes*, July 1986; and William Bryant Logan, "Rococo Rustic," *House & Garden*, November 1986.

2. Donna Warner and Donald Vining, "Adirondack Furniture," *Metropolitan Home*, March 1982, p. 79.

THE BACKGROUND: RUSTIC TASTE IN ENGLAND AND AMERICA

1. Christopher Hussey, *English Gardens and Landscapes, 1700–1750*, p. 45.

2. Eleanor von Erdberg, *Chinese Influences on European Garden Structures*, pp. 54, 114; William Marshall, *On Planting and Rural Ornament*, 3rd ed., 2 vols. (London, 1803), I:258. See also Peter Hunt, *The Book of Garden Ornament*, p. 168.

3. Morrison Heckscher, "Eighteenth-Century Rustic Furniture Designs," *Furniture History*, 1975, p. 59.

4. Robert Manwaring, *The Chair-Maker's Guide* (London, 1766), preface.

5. Marshall, *On Planting and Rural Ornament*, I:302.

6. Charles McIntosh, *The Book of the Garden*, 2 vols. (Edinburgh, 1853), I:706.

7. Ibid., I:713.

8. Ibid., I:687–88.

9. Ibid., I:678.

10. Ibid., I:687–88.

11. Two examples were the work of the influential John Claudius Lodoun: *The Encyclopedia of Gardening* (1819) and *The Gardener's Magazine*, which he edited. For other primary printed material, consult the chronological bibliographies in the following: Eleanor Sinclair Rohde, *The Story of the Garden*, p. 278ff., and the magazine *Garden and Forest* for 12 March 1890, pp. 131–35.

12. Selim, "On Rustic-work as Garden Ornaments," *The Gardener's Magazine*, 1834, p. 486.

13. McIntosh, *The Book of the Garden*, I:692. See also Esther Mipaas, "Cast-Iron Furnishings," *American Art & Antiques*, May–June 1979, pp. 34–41; and Margot Gayle, "Cast-Iron Architecture, U.S.A.," *Historic Preservation*, January–March 1975, pp. 15–19.

14. Fiske Kimball, *Mr. Samuel McIntire, Carver* (Salem, Massachusetts, 1940, reprinted 1966), pp. 75–76.

15. Andrew Jackson Downing, *A Treatise on the Theory and Practice of Landscape Gardening*, p. 398.

Notes

16. John W. Barber and Henry Howe, *Historical Collections of the State of New York* (New York, 1845), pp. 64–65. Hornby Lodge was brought to my attention by Mary Ellen Domblewski.

17. Alf Evers, *The Catskills, from Wilderness to Woodstock* (Garden City, New York, 1972), p. 402.

18. Achille Murat, *America and the Americans* (New York, 1849), p. 95; William Nathaniel Banks, "The Wesleyan Grove Campground on Martha's Vineyard," *Antiques*, July 1983, pp. 104–15; and Floyd and Marion Rinhart, *Summertime: Photographs of Americans at Play* (New York, 1978), p. 182.

19. Clarence C. Cook, *A Description of the New York Central Park*, p. 15.

20. Cook's *Description*, cited above, is still the best single primary source of information about the founding and early years of Central Park.

21. "Structures in Rustic Work," *American Agriculturist*, December 1870, p. 458; Cook, *Description*, p. 120. Julian Munckwitz is mentioned by Robert Hale Newton, "Our Summer Resort Architecture: An American Phenomenon and Social Document," *Art Quarterly*, I (Autumn, 1941): 307.

22. *The New York Illustrated News*, 22 June 1860.

23. Henry Hudson Holly, *Holly's Country Seats*, p. 60.

24. William C. Tweed, Laura E. Souilliere, and Henry G. Law, *National Park Service Rustic Architecture, 1916–42;* Albert H. Good, *Park and Recreation Structures*, II:96–97.

25. William S. Wicks, *Log Cabins and Cottages: How to Build and Furnish Them*.

26. John Burroughs, "Wildlife About my Cabin," *Century Magazine*, August 1899.

27. Natale Curtis, "The New Log House at Craftsman Farms; An Architectural Development of the Log Cabin," *The Craftsman*, November 1911, p. 196.

28. Bliss Carman, "The Ghost House: A Quiet Day in the Catskills," *The Craftsman*, June 1906, p. 282.

29. *Country Life in America*, 12 April 1912, pp. 19–20, 56.

30. Henry H. Saylor, *Bungalows*, p. 153.

31. George Leland Hunter, "Summer Furniture," *Country Life in America*, 15 May 1912, p. 64. See also James Collier Marshall, "Furnishing of the Bungalow," *Country Life in America*, September 1914, pp. 45–48.

AN ADIRONDACK AESTHETIC: FROM SHANTY TO GREAT CAMP

1. William Dix, "Summer Life in Luxurious Adirondack Camps," *The Independent*, 2 July 1903, p. 1156.

2. Alice Kellogg, "Luxurious Adirondack Camps," *Broadway Magazine*, August 1908, p. 208.

3. Raymond Spears, "The New Adirondacks," *The Outlook*, 24 May 1916, p. 193.

4. [J. P. Lundy], *The Saranac Exiles: A Winter's Tale of the Adirondacks* (Philadelphia, 1880), p. 122.

5. "Chronicle," diary of Dr. Arpad Gerster, 1895–98, p. 122. The Adirondack Museum Library.

6. Typescript of an article from the Glens Falls *Republican*, 1859. The Adirondack Museum Library.

7. Anonymous correspondent in *The Spirit of the Times*, 15 July 1848.

8. Reverend Henry Smith Huntington, diary entry for 15 July 1853. The Adirondack Museum Library, microfilm 4.60, pp. 245–246.

9. "The People of the State of New York against Frederick Hasbrouck," typed transcript of a hearing before the State Supreme Court, Raquette Lake Hotel, 19 June 1906, vol. 5, p. 260. The Adirondack Museum Library. Snyder Papers.

10. See Craig Gilborn, *Durant: The Fortunes and Woodland Camps of a Family in the Adirondacks.*

11. Seneca Ray Stoddard, *The Adirondacks, Illustrated* (Glens Falls, New York, 1888), p. 206.

12. Alfred L. Donaldson, *A History of the Adirondacks*, 2 vols. (New York, 1921), II:91–92.

13. Witness testimony, "The People of the State of New York against Joseph A. Ladew," 1903, typed transcript. The Adirondack Museum Library. Snyder Papers.

14. Typed excerpt of a reminiscence of Mrs. John Pruyn of Albany, recorded in the summer of 1894. The Adirondack Museum Library.

15. Its direct descendant is the present firm of Wareham–DeLair in Saranac Lake.

16. Interview with Jacques DeMattos, 15 January 1970. The Adirondack Museum Library.

17. Joseph F. Grady, *The Adirondacks: The Story of a Wilderness* (Old Forge, New York, 1933), p. 257.

18. Augustus Shepard, *Camps in the Woods*, p. 28.

19. Henry Wellington Wack, "Kamp Kill Kare," *Field and Stream*, February 1903, pp. 651–61.

ADIRONDACK TREE FURNITURE

1. Elizabeth Putnam McIver, "Early Days at Putnam Camp," a paper printed in September 1941. The Adirondack Museum Library.

2. Ernest Ingersoll, reporting a visit to Slabsides, in "John Burroughs at West Park," *The New York Times Saturday Review of Books and Art*, 27 August 1898, p. 568.

3. See E. H. Ketchledge, *Trees of the Adirondack High Peak Region* (Glens Falls, New York, 1979), pp. 50–54; and Joseph S. Illick, *Common Trees of New York* (Washington, D.C., 1927), p. 40. Cedar taxonomy: Northern white, also known as American arborvitae, *Thuja occidentalis;* Eastern red, *Juniperus virginiana;* and Atlantic (or Southern) white, *Chamaecyparis thyoides.*

4. "A Rustic Flower Stand," *American Agriculturist*, January 1869, p. 23.

5. Gertrude Atherton, *The Aristocrats, Being the Impressions of the Lady Helen Pole* (London: John Lane, 1901), p. 12.

6. W. W. Durant to John Callahan, 29 June 1899. Letterbook, The Adirondack Museum Library.

7. G. M. Hoppin, "The Adirondack Lakes," *Broadway, A London Magazine*, March–August 1869, p. 266.

8. *Eighth and Ninth Reports of the Forest, Fish and Game Commission* (Albany, New York, 1903), pp. 277–78. See also Anonymous, "The Destruction of Young Spruce for Rustic Architecture," *Woods and Waters*, Winter 1903–4, pp. 14–15.

9. The auction took place at Christie's, New York, 12 December 1986. See the catalogue *19th-Century Decorative Arts*, 12 December 1986, lots 261 and 264.

10. Selim, "On Wooden Rustic-work as Garden Ornaments," *The Gardener's Magazine*, 1834, pp. 485–89.

11. Mildred Phelps Stokes, *Camp Chronicles* (Blue Mountain Lake, New York, 1964), p. 14.

12. John L. Cunningham, *Three Years with the Adirondack Regiment* (Glens Falls, New York, 1920), p. 94.

13. *The Boonville Herald*, 12 June 1895, p. 1.

14. *Wilderness Homes: A Book of the Log Cabin* (New York, 1908), p. 101.

15. Furniture made from the horns of longhorn cattle was popular in late-nineteenth-century America; Tiffany's in New York City sold it. One of the masters of the craft was Wenzel Friedrich (1827–1902), an emigrant from Bohemia, who began to manufacture horn furniture in 1880 in San Antonio, Texas. See Johnathan Fairbanks and Elizabeth Bidwell Bates, *American Furniture: 1620 to the Present* (New York, 1981), pp. 427, 452; and Richard St. John, *Longhorn Artist, Wenzel Friedrich* (Wichita, Kansas, 1982). For a general discussion, see Simon Jervis, "Antler and Horn Furniture," *Victoria and Albert Museum Year Book* (London, 1972).

COTTAGE AND BUNGALOW FURNITURE

1. Interview with Frances T. Brown, Indianapolis, 27 January 1974, and letters from Brown to the author, 12 May 1976 and 24 November 1977.

2. Letters from Mary J. Neal, former bookkeeper at the company, to the author, 8 January and 22 August 1974.

3. "Hickory Furniture for Country Houses and Living Gardens," *The Craftsman*, July 1913, p. 450.

4. *Rustic Old Hickory* (Martinsville, Indiana, 1902), pp. 36–37.

5. A fancy willow rocker appears in a photograph taken by Walker Evans, *Coal Miner's House, Scotts Run, West Virginia*, 1935, reproduced in *Walker Evans, First and Last* (New York, 1978), p. 113. See also David A. Hanks, *Innovative Furniture in America* (New York, 1981), p. 62.

6. Elmo and Mark Stoll, *Pioneer Catalogue of Country Living* (Toronto, n.d.), pp. 103–4. See also *A Pioneer Catalogue* (Belle Center, Ohio, c. 1982), p. 5.

7. See "A Whispered Invitation to 'Set Awhile,' " *The Case Western Reserve Magazine*, November–December 1980, p. 42. Other modern chair makers, according to David Luthy, director of the Amish Historical Library in Aylmer, Ontario, include John Martin, Aylmer; Henry B. Yoder, Charm, Ohio; and Amos Zook and sons, Somerset County, Pennsylvania. Luthy to author, 25 December 1982, and 14 January 1984.

8. An Amish bentwood rocker was included in the Whitney Museum of American Art's 1985 exhibition "High Styles." See Lisa Phillips *et al.*, *High Styles: Twentieth-Century American Design* (New York, 1985), pp. 70–71.

9. See Marilyn Bethany, "Barking Up the Right Tree," *The New York Times Magazine*, 20 June 1982, p. 64.

10. Information about the Mottville enterprises has been culled from documents, catalogues, and clippings in the library of the Onondaga Historical Association, Syracuse.

11. [Francis A. Sinclair], *Illustrated Circular and Pricelist . . . of the Union Chair Works* (Mottville, New York, 1876).

12. *Syracuse Herald Journal*, 5 and 14 January 1943.

13. *Catalogue No. 45* (Mottville, New York, n.d.), p. 3.

14. Elizabeth Richards to author, 10 April 1979.

15. Robert Judson Clark, ed., *The Arts and Crafts Movement in America, 1876–1916* (Princeton, New Jersey, 1972), p. 38.

16. Harold Donald Eberlein, *The Practical Book of Interior Decoration* (Philadelphia, 1919), p. 201, quoted in John Crosby Freeman, *Forgotten Rebel: Gustav Stickley*, University of Delaware Master's Thesis, June 1965, pp. 49–50.

17. George Leland Hunter, "Summer Furniture," *Country Life in America*, 15 May 1912.

18. John Crosby Freeman, *Forgotten Rebel*, p. 3.

19. The discussion of the Westport chair is based on the following letters, at the Adirondack Museum: Mary Lee to Mary Marquand Hochschild, 11 August 1962; Mary Lee to author, 14 March and 12 August 1974. Charles F. Montgomery called to my attention the similarity of the Westport chair to Rietveld's Red-Blue chair in 1976. An article on Rietveld includes an illustration of a Westport chair captioned "Early Do-it-yourselfer, c. 1915," but the date is misleading as the chair actually dates from 1904, ten years before Rietveld designed his chair. See Scott Burton, "Furniture Journal: Rietveld," *Art in America*, November 1980, pp. 102–8.

FROM OLD-TIME RUSTIC WORKERS TO CONTEMPORARY CRAFTSMEN

1. Marc Cook, *The Wilderness Cure* (New York, 1881), p. 44.

2. Seneca Ray Stoddard, *The Adirondacks, Illustrated* (Glens Falls, New York, 1893), p. 202.

Here are listed works relating to rustic furniture making and rustic taste in America. The best sources for studying rustic taste and styles in America are the many magazines that catered to an interest in horticulture, agriculture, and country living in late-nineteenth- and early-twentieth-century America, including: *American Agriculturist*, *Country Life in America*, *The Craftsman*, *The Gardener's Monthly*, *The Horticulturist*, and *Indoors and Out*. Articles cited from these magazines below only hint at what is available to the researcher, especially as far as illustrations are concerned.

Aldrich, Chilson. *The Real Log Cabin* (New York, 1928).

Ames, Joseph B. "Building a Log Cabin," *Country Life in America*, 15 May 1912, pp. 62, 82.

Bailey, M. Kennedy. "A Forest House," *The Craftsman*, May 1911, pp. 205–07.

Beals, Jessie Tarbox. "An Open Camp in the Woods," *Country Life in America*, June 1910, p. 204.

———. "Bungalows of All Types for Hill and Dale," *Country Life in America*, September 1914, pp. 38–41.

Beard, D. C. *Shelters, Shacks, and Shanties* (New York, 1914).

Boyd, Charles Vaughan. "The Old-Fashioned Log Cabin," *Woman's Home Companion*, May 1916, p. 46.

Brimmer, Frank Everett. *Camps, Log Cabins, Lodges and Clubhouses* (New York, 1925).

Bryant, William Cullen, ed. *Picturesque America; Or, The Land We Live In*, 2 vols. (New York, 1872).

Burroughs, Julian. "How I Built My Own Country House," *Country Life in America*, February 1906, pp. 415–17.

Butterfield, W. H. "The Why and Wherefore of Bungalow Construction," *Country Life in America*, September 1914, pp. 53–55.

Carman, Bliss. "The Ghost House: A Quiet Day in the Catskills," *The Craftsman*, June 1906, pp. 279–85.

Carpenter, Warwick S. "How to Build a Recreation Log Cabin," *Recreation*, July 1909, pp. 17–19, 32–33.

Cleaveland, Nehemiah. *Green-Wood Cemetery: A History of the Institution from 1838 to 1864* (New York, 1866).

Cook, Clarence C. *A Description of the New York Central Park* (New York, 1869, reprinted 1972).

———. "Central Park," *Scribner's Monthly*, September 1873, pp. 523–29.

Cooper, William. *Illustrated Catalogue of Goods Manufactured and Supplied by . . . Iron Building and Rustic Works* (London, n.d. [c. 1900]).

"A Craftsman Lodge for the Wilderness," *The Craftsman*, October 1916, pp. 82–88.

"Craftsman Summer Log Houses," *The Craftsman*, August 1911, pp. 506–11.

Crosby, Ernest. "The Century of Ugliness," *The Craftsman*, July 1904, pp. 409–10.

Curtis, Natale. "The New Log House at Craftsman Farms: An Architectural Development of the Log Cabin," *The Craftsman*, November 1911, pp. 196–203.

Dix, William Frederick. "Summer Life in Luxurious Adirondack Camps," *The Independent*, 2 July 1903, pp. 1556–62.

Downing, A. J. *A Treatise on the Theory and Practice of Landscape Gardening, Adapted to North America* (New York, 1875, reprinted 1977).

Dunne & Co. "Landscape Architects, Rustic Builders," catalogue (New York, 1902).

Dwyer, C. P. *The Immigrant Builder, Or, Practical Hints to Handy-Men* (Philadelphia, 1872).

Ellis, Raymond A. "Bungalows of Logs," *Indoors and Out*, No. 6, 1906, pp. 300–304.

————. "The Cheapest House—The Log Cabin," *Country Life in America*, 15 April 1912, pp. 39–41.

Fernald, Benjamin G. "The Decorative Possibilities of Birch and Cedar Bark," *Country Life in America*, 1 August 1911, pp. 53–54.

Fisher, Theodore M. "Rustic Architecture at its Best," *Country Life in America*, April 1909, pp. 643–44.

Ford, E. Drusille. "The Environment of a Country Home," *The Craftsman*, June 1908, pp. 280–88.

"A Forest Bungalow," *The Craftsman*, June 1904, pp. 305–309.

"The Forest Pavilion at the Paris Exposition," *Garden and Forest*, 2 October 1889, p. 478; 9 October 1889, pp. 490–91; 15 January 1890, pp. 26–27.

French, Lillie Hamilton. "Adirondack Camps," *Harper's Bazaar*, 16 September 1899.

"Furniture and Rural Structures of Iron," *Illustrated Annual Register of Rural Affairs*, 1858–60, pp. 153–59.

"Furniture for Piazza and Lawn," *Indoors and Out*, No. 3, 1906, p. 147.

Gaut, Helen Lukens. "The Charm and Usefulness of a Mountain Camp," *The Craftsman*, August 1910, pp. 593–96.

Good, Albert H. *Park and Recreation Structures:* Part 1. *Administration and Basic Service Facilities;* Part 2. *Recreational and Cultural Facilities;* Part 3. *Overnight and Organized Camp Facilities* (National Park Service, Washington, D.C., 1938).

Grout, A. J. "A Log Cabin in Vermont, *Country Life in America*, 15 May 1912, pp. 59–60.

Harris, William Laurel. "Rustic Life and the Furniture It Demands," *Good Furniture*, October 1915, pp. 228–32.

Hasluck, Paul N., ed. *Rustic Carpentry* (Philadelphia, 1907). Articles anthologized from *Work, An Illustrated Magazine of Practice and Theory for All Workmen, Professional and Amateur*, 6 April 1889–5 December 1891.

Hibberd, Shirley. *Rustic Adornments for Homes of Taste* (London, 1856).

"Hints About Fences," *American Agriculturist*, August 1866, p. 285.

Holly, Henry Hudson. *Holly's Country Seats* (New York, 1863).

Holman, E. E. *Picturesque Camps, Cabins and Shacks* (Philadelphia, 1908).

"Home-made Fancy Baskets," *American Agriculturist*, December 1869.

"Hospitality to Our Friends the Birds," *American Agriculturist*, March 1869, p. 100.

"Household Ornaments," *American Agriculturist*, February 1868, p. 65.

Hunt, Ben W. *How to Build and Furnish a Log Cabin* (New York, 1974). [Combines books published in 1939 and 1947.]

Hunter, George Leland. "Summer Furniture," *Country Life in America*, 15 May 1912.

"Illustrations of Ornamental Iron Work," *The Horticulturist*, February 1856, p. 115.

Jersey Keystone Wood Co. *Rustic Cedar Furniture*, catalogue (Trenton, N.J., n.d. [c. 1910]).

Kellogg, Alice M. "Recent Camp Architecture" [in two parts], *International Studio*, 1905, pp. 73–76; 1906, pp. 6–10.

———. "Luxurious Adirondack Camps," *Broadway Magazine*, August 1908, pp. 207–12.

Kelly, Florence Finch. "How to Furnish a Bungalow," *Indoors and Out*, August 1907, pp. 217–20.

Kemp, Oliver. "A Log Cabin for You," *Field and Stream*, July 1902.

———. *Wilderness Homes: A Book of the Log Cabin* (New York, 1908).

Lay, Charles Downing. "Gazebos and Summer Houses," *Indoors and Out*, No. 3, 1906, pp. 129–32.

"A Log Cabin Club House," *The Craftsman*, August 1916, pp. 523–24.

Marshall, James Collier. "Furnishing the Bungalow," *Country Life in America*, September 1914, pp. 45–48.

Martin, George A. *Our Homes; How to Beautify Them* (New York, 1888).

Mason, Bernard S. and Frederic H. Kock, *Cabins, Cottages, and Summer Homes* (New York, 1947).

Meinecke, Conrad E. *Your Cabin in the Woods* (Buffalo, 1945).

———. *Cabincrafts and Outdoor Living* (Buffalo, 1947).

[Lewis Miller], *Lewis Miller's Guide to Central Park* (Dearborn, Mich., 1977).

"Miniature Rustic Plant Stand," *American Agriculturist*, February 1863, p. 52.

Mitchell, Donald Grant. *Rural Studies with Hints for Country Places* (New York, 1867).

"Country Seats and Parks," *The New York Illustrated News*, 22 June 1860.

[O'Brien Brothers], *Illustrated Catalogue of O'Brien Bro's Rustic Designs* (Yonkers, N.Y., 1874).

Pike, Horace L. "Building a $600 Log Cabin," *Country Life in America*, June 1906, pp. 333–34.

Popular Science Publishing Co. *How To Build Cabins and Ranch Houses: with Complete Directions and Plans for Interiors, Furniture* (New York, 1952).

Priestman, Dorothy Tuke. "Furnishings for the Bungalow," *Country Life in America*, February 1911, pp. 321–23.

"A Real Lesson in House Building," *The Craftsman*, June 1906, pp. 408–12.

Rice, Berkeley. "The Education of a Country Craftsman" [Ken Heitz], *USAIR*, July 1983, pp. 62–67.

"Rockwork and Rustic Objects," *Illustrated Annual Register of Rural Affairs*, 1858–60, pp. 247–50.

"Rural Embellishments," *American Agriculturist*, 1865, pp. 217–18.

"Rustic Adornments," *The Gardener's Monthly*, November 1860, pp. 320, 338–39.

"A Rustic Carte de Visite Frame," *American Agriculturist*, February 1864, p. 53.

"A Rustic Flower Stand," *American Agriculturist*, January 1869, p. 23.

"Rustic Furniture," *The Horticulturist*, July 1858, pp. 304–306; August 1858, pp. 360–61.

"Rustic Furniture Especially Appropriate for the Informal Garden," *The Craftsman*, June 1913, pp. 349–52.

"Rustic Ornaments," *The Horticulturist*, 1855, pp. 353–55.

"A Rustic Seat," *American Agriculturist*, May 1864, p. 149.

"Rustic Seats and Structures," *Illustrated Annual Register of Rural Affairs*, 1855–57, pp. 302–307.

Rutstrum, Calvin. *The Wilderness Cabin* (New York, 1961).

Saylor, Henry H. *Bungalows* (New York, 1911).

Shepard, Augustus D. *Camps in the Woods* (New York, 1931).

Sloan, Samuel. *The Model Architect* (Philadelphia, 1852).

Smith, John M. "Rustic Adornments," *The Gardener's Monthly*, May 1860, pp. 131–33.

"Some Camp Furniture," *The Craftsman*, April 1908, pp. 106–11.

"The Spread of the Country Life Idea," *Country Life in America*, 15 April 1912, pp. 19–20.

"Structures in Rustic Work," *American Agriculturist*, December 1870, p. 458.

"A Summer Home," *The Craftsman*, May 1904, pp. 177–80.

Swanson, William Elmer. *Log Cabins* (New York, 1948).

"Three Craftsman Log Houses," *The Craftsman*, March 1907, pp. 742–55.

"Types of Woodland Camps," *Country Life in America*, 22 August 1908, p. 12.

Wack, Henry Wellington. "Kamp Kill Kare," *Field and Stream*, February 1903, pp. 651–61.

Wheeler, Gervase. *Rural Homes; Or Sketches of Houses Suited to Rural Life* (New York, 1851).

White, John P. *A Complete Catalogue of Garden Furniture and Garden Ornament* (London, 1906).

Whitton, L. C. "The St. Regis Camps," *Forest and Stream*, 18 June 1891, pp. 36, 435.

Wicks, William S. *Log Cabins and Cottages: How to Build and Furnish Them* (New York, 1889).

Williams, Henry T., and C. S. Jones. *Beautiful Homes, Or Hints in House Furnishing* (New York, 1878).

General works relating to the history of rustic furniture:

Baltrusaitus, Jurgis. *Aberrations, Quatre Essais sur la Légende des Formes* (Oliver Perrin, 1957).

Beeker, Bruce, and Jeff Parsons. "Adirondack Chair," *Fine Woodworking*, May–June 1985, pp. 46–49.

Brookhouse, Karol K. "Artistry in Willow," *Country Home*, June 1985, pp. 87–93.

Butler, Joseph. "American Mid-Victorian Outdoor Furniture," *Antiques*, June 1959, pp. 564–67.

Conroy, Dennis. "Artistry in Wood," *Adirondac*, August 1983, pp. 5–9.

Evers, Alf, and others, *Resorts of the Catskills* (New York, 1979).

Gayle, Margot. "Cast-Iron Architecture U.S.A.," *Historic Preservation*, January–March 1975, pp. 15–19.

Germann, Georg. *Gothic Revival in Europe and Britain*, trans. Gerald Onn (Cambridge, Mass., 1973).

Griswold, Ralph E. "Early American Garden Houses," *Antiques*, July 1970, pp. 82–87.

Heckscher, Morrison. "Eighteenth-Century Rustic Furniture Designs," *Furniture History*, 1975, pp. 59–65.

Herrmann, Wolfgang. *Laugier and Eighteenth Century French Theory* (London, 1962).

Hunt, Peter. ed. *The Book of Garden Ornament* (New York, 1981).

Hussey, Christopher. *English Gardens and Landscapes, 1700–1750* (New York, 1967).

Jarrett, David. *The English Landscape Garden* (New York, 1978).

Jervis, Simon. "Antler and Horn Furniture," *Victoria and Albert Museum Year Book*, 1972, pp. 87–99.

Jones, Barbara. *Follies & Grottoes* (London, 1953).

Kaiser, Harvey. *Great Camps of the Adirondacks* (Boston, 1982).

Keswick, Maggie. *The Chinese Garden* (New York, 1978).

Lancaster, Clay. *The Japanese Influence in America* (New York, 1963).

Limerick, Jeffrey W. "The Grand Resort Hotels of America," *Perspecta 15* (Yale School of Architecture, 1975).

Lovejoy, Arthur O. "The Chinese Origin of Romanticism" and "The First Gothic Revival and the Return to Nature," in *Essays in the History of Ideas* (Baltimore, 1948).

Mipass, Esther. "Cast-Iron Furnishings," *American Art and Antiques*, May–June 1979, pp. 34–41.

Newton, Roger Hale. "Our Summer Resort Architecture," *Art Quarterly*, Autumn 1941, pp. 297–318.

Pevsner, Nikolas, ed. *The Picturesque Garden and Its Influence Outside the British Isles* (Washington, D.C., 1974). [See essays by S. Lang and Marcia Allentuck.]

Robinson, D., D. Rosen, and A. Jaroslow. "Rustic Shelter: How Conservators Rebuilt a Traditional Summer House in Central Park," *Fine Homebuilding*, 1984, pp. 66–68.

Rohde, Eleanor Sinclair. *The Story of the Garden* (Boston, [1932]).

Rykwert, Joseph. *On Adam's House in Paradise: The Idea of the Primitive Hut in Architectural Theory* (New York, 1972).

Shepard, Paul. *Man In The Landscape* (New York, 1967).

Stephenson, Sue Honaker. *Rustic Furniture* (New York, 1979).

Stern, Robert A. M., ed. *The Anglo-American Suburb* (London, 1981).

Tweed, William C., Laura E. Soulliere, and Henry G. Law. *National Park Service Rustic Architecture: 1916–1942* (National Park Service, 1977). [Multilithed report.]

Von Erdberg, Eleanor. *Chinese Influences on European Garden Structures* (Cambridge, Mass., 1936).

Weslager, Clinton Alfred. *The Log Cabin in America* (Brunswick, N.J., 1969).

Wiebenson, Dora. *The Picturesque Garden in France* (Princeton, N.J., 1978).

Numbers refer to figures. Colorplates are indicated by italics.

The author and publisher would like to thank the following for permitting the reproduction of furniture, vintage photographs, and other works from their collections, as well as for providing access to their premises for photography. The credits for furniture in public collections appear in the captions:

Adirondack Museum Photograph [AMP], 4, 5, 29, 32, 33, 35, 39, 41–45, 47, 49, 52, 85, 88, 95, 109, 129, 135, 139, 151, 157, 162–164, 238, 244, 250, 253, 257, 260, 285–287, 289, 302; AMP. Gift of John Beals, 6; AMP. Gift of Franklin Brandreth, 1, 192, 303; AMP. Gift of Mrs. John Hancock, 265; AMP. Gift of Whitelaw Reid, 150; AMP. Gift of Mrs. Jacqueline Schonbrun and Sons in memory of Stanley I. Schonbrun, 37; AMP. Gift of Sidney Wheeler, 237; Mr. and Mrs. Donald Ballantine, 141; Mr. and Mrs. Thomas T. Bissell, 40, 208–210; Major and Mrs. C. V. Bowes, 68, 80, 248; Mrs. Morison Garrett Brigham, 10; James C. Brown, 293, 294; Bruce Crary Foundation, 19; Clara O. Bryere, 180, 224, 288; Joseph T. Butler, 16, 17; Camp Uncas, 143, *1, 25*; Hilda L. Champney, 301; Mr. and Mrs. Richard Cohen, 249; Mrs. John Collins, Sr., 197; Bruce N. Coulter, 46; The Detroit Institute of Arts. Founder's Society Purchase, William H. Murphy Fund, 23; Bill Distin, 48; Robert and Clair Doyle, 61; Mr. and Mrs. John Droz, Jr., 232–233; Echo Camp for Girls, 218; Preston Ewing, 84; Mr. and Mrs. Richard Fay, 245, *44*; Mrs. Francis P. Garvan, 125, 128, 129, 142–147, 155, 225–228; Albert Gates, 282; Edward Griffin, 114–116; Hampshire's of Dorking, England, *21*; Mrs. John Hancock, 270; Henry Ford Museum and Greenfield Village, Deerfield, Mich., 26; Henry Francis DuPont Winterthur Museum Library, Winterthur, Del., 3, 8, 9, 12–14; Hirschl & Adler Folk, New York, 65, 69, 185; Mrs. Walter Hochschild, 153, 154, *22, 23, 26, 27*; Harry Inman, 187, 188; Roger J. Jakubowski, *6 9, 40, 41*; Lee G. Jaques, 92; Mr. and Mrs. Joseph Kozma, 290–292; Land of the Oneidas, Boy Scouts of America, 136, 193; Mrs. Jean LeCompe, 75; Mary Lee, 275; Sheila Mackintosh, 53, 258, 262–264; Mr. and Mrs. Paul Maloney, 100; Margaret Woodbury Strong Museum, Rochester, 83; The Metropolitan Museum of Art, New York. Gift of Mrs. Sheila Riddell, in memory of Sir Percival David, 11; Herbert F. Mitchell Collection, 21; Museum of the City of New York, 27; Nettie Marie Jones Fine Arts Library, Lake Placid, New York, 70–73, 79, 93; The New York Historical Association, Cooperstown, 252; The New-York Historical Society, New York, 7, 189; The North Woods Club, Minerva, New York, *20, 49*; Onondaga Historical Association, Syracuse, 251; The Pope Family, *24*; Mr. and Mrs. Arthur Potter, 107, 201, 206, *38*; Mark Potter, 105; Mrs. Helen Gardner Powers and Mrs. Nancy Gardner Whalen, 183; Peter Read, 300; Whitelaw Reid Collection, *30*; Molly Rockwell, 243; Mrs. Robert W. Searle, 220, 256, *43*; Mr. and Mrs. Craig Smith, 96, 97, 261; Mrs. Frederick Snyder Squier, 54, 55, 140, 158; Earl and Clarice Stanyon, 67; Richard Storrs, 138, 204; SUNY Cortland Outdoor Education Center, Camp Pine Knot, 99, 108, 110–113, 117, 123, 124, 161, 181, 182, 194, 198, 202, 217, 255, *2, 5, 29, 31, 45*; Ann Talmage, 127; Mr. and Mrs. Robb Tyler, 60, 81, 102, 106, 203, 207, 214; Marie Vallance, 160; Irving D. Vann, 317; Richard VanYperen, 159, 236, 237, *28*; Mr. and Mrs. Robert Webb, 247; William Wessels, 259; Mr. and Mrs. C. V. Whitney, 190–191; Barrie and Deedee Wigmore, 130.

Credits

(continued next page)

The author and publisher would like to thank the following photographers:

James Fynmore, 151; Karen Halverson, *1–9, 13–16, 20, 22, 24–29, 31, 36–41, 43–46, 49, 50*; Bob Hanson, 299; Peter and Rosine Lemon, 36, 56–59, 62, 64, 74, 76–78, 84, 118–120, 134, 168, 173–178, 196, 219, 223, 231, 242, 245, 246, 266, 280–281; Richard Linke, 139, 147, 155, 225–228; Irving Stedman, 70–73, 93.

Photographs by Craig Gilborn: 2, 10, 19, 22, 25, 28, 31, 50, 53–55, 60, 61, 63, 66–68, 75, 80–82, 86, 87, 89–91, 94, 99–108, 110–117, 123, 124, 126, 127, 130–133, 136–138, 140–144, 146, 148, 152–154, 156–161, 163–167, 170–172, 181–184, 186, 187, 190, 191, 193–195, 198, 200–206, 209–218, 220–222, 224, 229, 230, 232–236, 239–241, 243, 247–249, 254–256, 258, 259, 261–264, 267–275, 277, 278, 283, 284, 295–298, 304–306, *10–12, 17–19, 21, 23, 30, 32–35, 42, 48*.